ON THE LESSON TEE

Basic Golf Fundamentals

JACK GROUT
Jack Nicklaus' Teacher and Coach

Illustrations By Jim McQueen

THE ATHLETIC INSTITUTE
NORTH PALM BEACH, FL 33408

A WORD FROM THE PUBLISHER

What? Another book on how to play golf?

That makes how many? At least 43,295, give or take a few thousand.

But wait! This is not just another book on how to play golf.

It is written primarily for the junior golfer, but it can be enjoyed just as much by the lifelong amateur.

And it was written by Jack Grout, who turned a 10-year-old boy in Columbus, Ohio, into perhaps the greatest player the game has ever known.

"Jack Grout stresses fundamentals," says that player, Jack Nicklaus.

But doesn't every teacher of golf? Or at least, aren't they supposed to?

Nicklaus explains the difference in Grout's method in his Forward on another page. In a word, it's simplicity, developed through Grout's years of an analytical approach to teaching the game.

And in addition to the usual well-illustrated pages on the game's fundamentals, this book also deals with such matters as course management and trouble shots, psychology and etiquette.

To ensure that the young reader's interest in the game is solidified, there are separate chapters on the history of golf and the evolution of its equipment, as well as many ancient photographs.

It makes for a marvelous package, a wonderful book for young golfers. It is a book we think golfers of all ages should enjoy.

Howard J. Bruns
President and Chief Executive Officer
The Athletic Institute

Dustin Cole
Executive Director
The Athletic Institute

FOREWORD

Jack Grout stresses fundamentals. He keeps them to a minimum, and he keeps them simple. I can assure you that the simplicity of Jack's approach is the major reason why I've managed to play as well as I have over the years.

Both the simplicity and the completeness of Jack's message come through in this book. You will also find that he never fails to explain to you — as he did to me — the reasons behind his recommendations. This is important in the long run because, as the great Bob Jones once observed, we really don't reach our maximum as players until we understand why we must do what we must do.

— Jack Nicklaus

CONTENTS

ACKNOWLEDGEMENTS

The Athletic Institute would like to acknowledge the contributions of knowledge and skills of the following:

Atheneum Publishers, Inc.
Glynn (Bud) Harvey
Jim McQueen
National Golf Foundation
P.G.A. Of America
U.S. Golf Association

INTRODUCTION

In this book I will not only tell you how to swing a golf club, and why you should do so in a particular way, but also how to better yourself as a player of the game. There is an art to practicing and taking lessons and learning from watching others. There is an art also to managing your game on the course — selecting the right club, planning your shots, saving strokes when things begin to go sour. And all these factors are just as important to your score as how you actually swing the club.

The more you play, the more you will appreciate the infinite variety of challenges that golf presents. You will find that every shot offers a different set of factors to be considered. The wind velocity and direction, the lie of the ball in the grass, the length of the shot, the terrain on which you stand, the softness or hardness of the fairway and the green, the trees, sand and water — all these things, and many more, affect how you perform every time you swing the club.

You will find that golf, unlike so many other activities in our daily lives, rewards success and penalizes failure *immediately*. You do not need to wait for a teacher or a professor to grade your efforts. In golf, you know as soon as the ball leaves the clubface whether or not you've performed well or poorly.

Golf is a game that brings out both the best and worst aspects of a person's character. It rewards patience, self-control and honest self-analysis. It penalizes anger and self-deception. It is a game that pits you alone against the course. And the course doesn't move around to block your shots, or try to knock you out of bounds, or throw you curve balls. It just sits there, passively, waiting for you to challenge it — and yourself. In other words, the burden of proof is solely on you, the player, which is one of the chief reasons it is such a popular and life-long game.

Also, golf is to some extent a game of luck. You will hit bad shots that finish next to the flagstick, and you will hit super shots that bounce into trouble. In either case, it will be up to you to accept the good and bad shots and take them in stride.

In some ways golf is a game of strength, but it's far more a game of rhythm, timing, finesse and mind over matter. It's a game in which short, slightly built men and women can excel. There are far more Davids than there are Goliaths in the ranks of the golf heroes.

Jack Grout

Two young Scottish sportsmen: an eighteenth century painting.

Credit: Jack Level

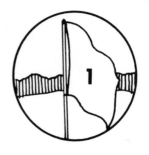

HOW IT ALL
GOT STARTED

The origin of the game of golf is an enigma wrapped in mystery. Generally, the game of golf is attributed to the Scots, a dour people who are suspected of developing the game as a special form of flagellation. And, after we examine all the other claims, we'll wind up back in Scotland with a shepherd boy banging a chunk of boxwood across the moor with his crook.

Some say the game evolved out of a game known to the Roman soldiers as "paganica" and brought by them to Britain. Other researchers argue that golf is a direct descendant of the Dutch game of "kolven" and was brought home from the Lowlands by Scottish mercenary soldiers. This school of thought supports its argument by pointing out that the Dutch game was played with a tool called a "kolf" which, in turn, traces its ancestry back to the German word, "kolbe," meaning club. Also, the kolven school points out that the language of the Dutch game offers additional clues. For instance, the Dutch game uses the expression, "Stuit mij!" — meaning "It stops me", which corresponds in sound and sense to the golf expression "stymie", meaning a blockage by one ball of a second ball.

Also, the old Dutch game offers another expression: "Vooor!" It certainly sounds like the familiar warning cry of "Fore!" used by the golfer to warn others of a flying ball.

For all this similarity, the proponents of this argument have failed to win many converts. Why? Because "kolven" was a game played on a court (or on ice-bound canals in the winter), using large balls and instruments that looked more like modern hockey sticks than golf clubs.

Still others suggest the game originated in France and was called "jeu de mail" which was transported to England as the game of "pall mall." It provided a name for one of London's better known thoroughfares. However, the similarity between "jeu de mail" and the modern game of golf is pretty remote. The French pastime is more closely related to croquet.

Actually, ball and bat games are as old as mankind. And whether golf is indigenous to Scotland or was smuggled into the country under dark of night makes little real difference to us. After all is said and done, we arrive back at that same bleak Scottish moor with the bored shepherd boy knocking a block of boxwood from one rabbit hole to another.

7

This much we know: Sometime early in the 15th century, the game inflamed the imagination of the Scots because in 1457, at the urging of King James II, the Scottish Parliament issued an Act which forbade the playing of football and golf, decreeing that "the futeball and golfe be utterly cryed downe and not be used." The reason: Scotland and England were in a perpetual state of war and James was worried that the Scots would lose their touch with the longbow. So he told them, in effect, to get their butts back to the archery butts.

But even a king couldn't stamp out the game of golf with a piece of paper. Some two hundred years later another Stuart king, Charles, was playing golf when a messenger brought him news of a fresh rebellion in Ireland. Charles is reported to have been so dismayed that he three-putted the next hole.

Meanwhile, like an epidemic that knows no national boundaries, the game of golf leaped the border and infected the English. However, again royalty played a key role in this transplantation. It was Mary, Queen of Scots, who introduced the word "caddie" to the game. During her extended residence in France, she had acquired the golf habit and resumed playing when she moved into Buckingham Palace with Henry. She was accompanied on her rounds by a club-carrying young gallant whom she addressed in her Parisian brogue as the "cadet", or "caddie."

The French source of golf has an added supporter in Professor Douglas Young whose history of St. Andrews, the ancient university town, claims that Scottish troops enlisting with the French to fight the English became converted to the French game of "chole" and brought it back with them. This would date the importation of golf into Scotland at about 1420. There is some reason to believe that "chole" was a legitimate ancestor of golf since it was played with iron-faced clubs and a crudely rounded wooden ball.

In any event, we find the game becoming popular in Scotland at about this period. And we find the earliest implements of the players consisted of roughly shaped balls of boxwood and crudely fashioned clubs of blackthorn. And as the border wars between England and Scotland gradually subsided, the Scottish bow-makers and arrow fletchers turned to club-making to supplement their income. This was a perfectly natural turn of events since the bowyers were intimately familiar with the characteristics of the wood they worked with and had the tools and the skills to shape and balance the clubs needed by the golfers.

A Rembrandt Etching

The Sport of Kolef

"Grand Golf Tournament by Professional

Players on Leith Links 1867''

"On The Lesson Tee"

Group of the most famous Golf Pros, taken at St. Andrews, 1856

The earliest golf balls were roughly hewn from chunks of boxwood which had the desirable characteristics of resiliency and durability. However, the wooden ball had limited "carry" and undesirable flight characteristics. It was the introduction of the "featherie" ball in the early part of the 17th century that won a host of new converts to the game. The "featherie" ball was constructed much in the fashion of a leather ball used by the old Romans for a game similar to handball. The cover consisted of two pieces of bull's hide that were stitched together, leaving open a small unstitched area into which the ball maker stuffed boiled chicken or goose feathers which expanded on drying to provide a tightly filled case. The accepted formula for one ball was "a hatful of feathers", meaning the volume of feathers which would fill the standard top hat of the day.

The "featherie" ball was substantially more expensive than the old chunk of boxwood since a ball maker, working diligently and staying away from the neighborhood pub, could produce no more than three or four balls a day. For this reason, the prudent Scots golfer was most reluctant to abandon his search for a lost ball, leading the early rules makers to set a time limit on the length of his search which tended to hold up play.

The game of golf took a quantum leap forward in popularity after 1843 when the discovery of gutta-percha was announced. It was a gum obtained from certain trees and shrubs found in the Dutch East Indies. In mid-century, the first gutta-percha balls began to take over the golf ball market. They were smoother, rounder and less expensive than the old featherie. They also flew farther than the featherie, but they had one fault which soon became apparent to the golfer. Their flight was quite erratic until they had acquired a few nicks and dents. This confirmed the suspicion of many players that the dynamics of flight were directly related to roughened, or uneven, surface. Now it became the custom to hand hammer the new gutta-percha ball to create a crude dimpling effect. As the modern ball evolved, this principle was applied in the form of "dimples", cross-hatching or other experimental surface markings.

The greater carrying distance of the new rubber ball and its truer flight increased the attraction of the game. At about the same period, another ball, of balata, appeared on the market. This material, from Central and South America, had a consistency of rubber but was more resinous than gummy and lacked the resiliency of the gutty ball.

It remained for a chemist named Samuel Coburn Haskell in 1898 to produce a revolutionary golf ball with a solid rubber core around which was wound rubber thread under great tension. The ball then was covered with gutta-percha and the cover scored with geometric markings to produce longer and better controlled flight. The Haskell ball was the great-grand-daddy of the modern golf ball and was produced in such quantities as to bring the price of golf balls within the range of the average person. It led directly to the explosive growth of popularity of the game in the early years of the present century.

A number of experiments were made with different centers for the Haskell ball. The solid rubber core was replaced by steel spheres, glass spheres and even balloon sacs filled with various kinds of paste. Meanwhile, matching experiments with different surface scorings finally evolved into the standard dimple pattern which is characteristic of the modern golf ball.

The dimples perform an essential function. When struck by a golf club, the ball develops spin, and the revolving dimples set up a turbulence in the air which gives the ball added "lift" for longer flight. A smoothly rounded ball will tend to respond to the gravitational pull after a short flight of, perhaps, only 90-100 yards. On the other hand, the dimpled ball, rising on a cushion of air created by the turbulence, will carry an additional 150-200 yards.

The modern golf ball must meet the rigid specifications spelled out by the United States Golf Association in this country, by the Royal & Ancient Golf Club of St. Andrews in Britain. The USGA specifies that the golf ball shall weigh not more than 1.620 ounces ánd shall measure no less than 1.680 inches in diameter with a velocity after impact no greater than 250 feet per second as measured by the USGA testing apparatus. The British specifications are essentially the same although they will accept a slightly smaller ball (1.52 inches in diameter).

The manufacture of a golf ball is too detailed for discussion here, except to say they are designated by "compression" for marketing purposes. The PGA tournament professionals and extremely hard-hitting amateurs commonly use a "100 compression" golf ball. It requires tremendous impact force for maximum advantage. For the average male golfer, the 90 compression ball is most suitable. For the light hitters and women golfers, an 80 compression ball is best.

Although the ball developed by Haskell — consisting of a rubber core, tightly wound rubber thread and a balata or gutta-percha cover

Hand nicking and painting gutty balls.

— remains a standard of quality, a relatively new solid ball has captured a large share of the popular market because of its durability. The new solid ball, developed by a young chemical wizard about 15 years ago, is made from a synthetic elastomer derived from petroleum. It is virtually impossible to nick or cut it in the course of regular play, a weakness of the wound ball.

| Bramble 1899 | Mystery 1919 | Sweet Shot 1933 | Modern Ball |

Evolution of the Golf Club

Just as the golf ball has evolved from a rounded chunk of boxwood, so has the golf club evolved from shepherd's crook or crudely shaped blackthorn bole. It can be assumed that there was a period of experimentation with various types of wood before the earliest golfers determin-

ed that hickory provided the toughest shafts with minimum resistance to warp. The hickory golf shaft became the standard for clubmakers until the 1920s when the restless and inventive Americans became enamored of the game and started experimenting with new materials.

We will see how the introduction of the steel shaft and the matched sets of clubs changed the nature of golf and gave the American players an advantage over their British cousins that has continued to the present day.

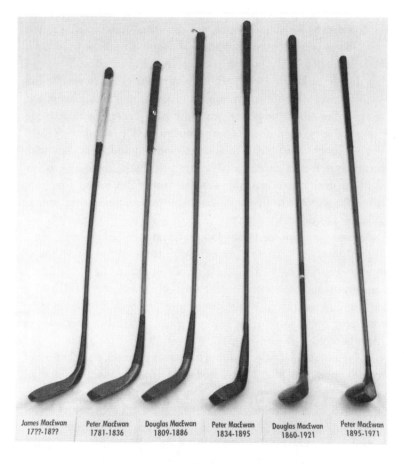

| James MacEwan | Peter MacEwan | Douglas MacEwan | Peter MacEwan | Douglas MacEwan | Peter MacEwan |
| 17??-18?? | 1781-1836 | 1809-1886 | 1834-1895 | 1860-1921 | 1895-1971 |

Antique Clubs

The early steel shafts of the 1920s and 1930s were made from low carbon tubular steel that had to be "carbonized" to provide the necessary strength for the relatively thin walls of the steel tube. We say "relatively thin" because those early steel shafts were a far cry from the modern light-weight steel tubing characteristic of the finer clubs on the market today. Those early steel shafts not only were thicker, but also heavier as a consequence, and lacked the "soft" feel of the hickory shaft.

The first steel shafts had no taper. That is, they didn't reduce in diameter between the grip and club head. Then, the shaft makers found that, by forcing the steel tube through a series of dies, they could reduce the diameter of the shaft. This was known as the "step-down" process.

Golfers, at first, were reluctant to abandon their hickory shafts for the new-fangled steel tools. But the steel shaft had obvious advantages that the old hickory shaft lacked. Hickory shafts varied in weight and flexibility and were subject to torsion. That is, they would twist and bend, or flex when the player struck the ball. These variations made it impossible for the clubmaker to produce a truly matched set of clubs — a set in which each club would feel and respond identically with the others in the set. Steel shafts, on the other hand, could be produced in quantities with matching characteristics. This meant that each club in the set could be swung with the same force to produce the desired range of distances.

It was the immortal Bobby Jones who popularized the steel shaft. At that time, the amateur code was rather fuzzy and Jones, although an amateur and a national sports hero, was employed by the Spalding company to promote the new steel-shafted "matched" sets. And in 1930 the U.S.G.A. and the R & A approved the steel shaft for their tournament play, removing the last marketing barrier and the sales of steel shafts boomed.

The numbering of golf clubs (from 1 to 9 for the standard set of irons and from 1 to 5 for the standard set of woods) is another American invention. Back home in Britain, where the game began, irons were designated by such colorful names as "mid-iron," "mashie," and "mashie-niblick" and "niblick." These are certainly more attractive names than "3-iron," "5-iron" or "6-iron." In this instance, the American passion for standardization was rather depressing.

The irons are commonly distinguished by the degree of loft on their faces. That means the angle at which they are laid back from the vertical. The No. 1 iron, for example, is almost straight-faced. As we move back down through the clubs we reach the 9-iron with a face that is laid back at an angle of 51 degrees from vertical. Theoretically, each club when swung with the same force will propel the ball a roughly fixed distance. The following table of distances and degrees of loft is worth your study:

Club	Average Distance		Degrees of Loft
Woods	**Men**	**Women**	
No. 1	220 yds.	190 yds.	11 degrees
No. 2(*)	210 yds.	180 yds.	14 degrees
No. 3	200 yds.	170 yds.	17 degrees
No. 4	190 yds.	160 yds.	20 degrees
No. 5	175 yds.	150 yds.	23 degrees
Irons			
No. 1(*)	190 yds.	160 yds.	19 degrees
No. 2	180 yds.	150 yds.	23 degrees
No. 3	170 yds.	140 yds.	27 degrees
No. 4	160 yds.	130 yds.	31 degrees
No. 5	150 yds.	120 yds.	35 degrees
No. 6	140 yds.	110 yds.	39 degrees
No. 7	130 yds.	100 yds.	43 degrees
No. 8	120 yds.	90 yds.	47 degrees
No. 9	110 yds.	80 yds.	51 degrees
Wedge	90 yds.	70 yds.	55 degrees

(*) Not commonly used, nor are the Nos. 10 and 11 irons

Before we leave the subject of club-making, let's answer the question: Why "bulge" on the face of the wood clubs?

The earliest golf clubs were commonly called "spoons," a name which persisted down to the Age of Numerology for the No. 3 wood. The original "driving club" became the "driver" and the "brassie" became the No. 2 wood, and so on. But the use of the word "spoon" is significant. Those early playing clubs actually were spoon-shaped; that is, they were concave.

As time wore on, golfing physicists discovered that concave striking surfaces weren't very efficient. They tended to distribute the force of the blow over a wider area, severely limiting the distance the ball would carry. Some unsung genius figured out that a convex "bulge" on the face of the club would concentrate the force of the clubface as it drove into the ball. The principle is much the same as applies to the baseball bat and ball. A flat board or a paddle won't knock a baseball much farther than the pitcher's mound. But a rounded bat of ash or hickory can knock a ball over the distant fence.

However, a perfectly rounded striking face meeting a round ball can result in a lot of foul balls. Early experiments with rounded faces on the wood clubs proved the player lost all control of direction. By trial and error, the club-makers arrived at the modest bulge which is now standard for most wood clubs.

And so the evolution of club-making has brought us to the modern matched sets of irons and woods. Developed in the United States, the matched sets of steel-shafted clubs (aluminum enjoyed a brief popularity in the late 1960s) have revolutionized the game as we know it.

The hickory-shafted club, which our British cousins were reluctant to abandon, was the tool of an artist rather than an engineer. Its "whippy" characteristics called for a looping, graceful swing arc. Shot-making with hickory shafts was an artistic triumph of the individual, each shot hand-tailored to the required distance and meeting the special conditions of play. On the other hand, a new breed of player in the United States, raised on the standardized steel shafts and matched sets, began to play an entirely different kind of a precision game — sometimes described by the Britons as "target golf."

The reference to "target golf" was directed partly at the machine-like precision of the American game and partly at the American custom of heavily watering their courses, especially the greens. The new breed of American player carefully calculated the distance to the green, set his precise swing machine, and flew the ball directly at the pin knowing that the backspin on the ball and the soft consistency of the turf would prevent the ball from bounding beyond the target.

This very precision of the American style, evolving out of the standardization of the club distances, became a characteristic of the American game. It also changed the teaching of golf from an exotic art form to a science. Only the psychological approach and the method of communicating made the teaching exercise a personal and individual one.

In this book we are going to follow very closely the path I took in instructing the young Jack Nicklaus when he was growing into the game as a youngster and a teenager. I believe you will find in it a simple and understandable explanation of the dynamics of the golf swing. And, again, I will remind you that there is no teaching until there is a corresponding "learning" at the other end — and learning requires concentration and hours of constructive practice. I can point the way and take you by the hand, but to reach your goal *you* must do the walking.

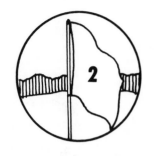

CONCEPTS OF
THE SWING

First, you should understand exactly what happens on a good golf shot. Imagine your ball is sitting on the grass and your target is a distant hole in the green marked by the flagstick. You want to strike the ball so it flies on a straight line to your target with enough carry to finish in the hole.

This straight line to the target is just that — your "target line." When you stand up to hit the shot, the area on your side of the target line is called "inside." The area on the other side of the line is "outside." The first requirement for a good golf shot is that your club's head be moving momentarily along that target line when it strikes the ball. If the clubhead is moving across the line in either direction at impact the shot cannot fly straight.

This is fundamental: Your shot will always *start out* in the direction your clubhead is moving when it strikes the ball. If your clubhead is cutting across this target line from the outside to the inside, the ball will start out to the left of the target if you are right-handed. If it's moving from the inside to outside the line, the ball has to start out to the right of the target. We'll assume you play golf right-handed.

You may ask: What's so difficult about swinging the clubhead straight down the line? Well, the complication is that you're standing to one side of the ball as you swing. This means that, to some degree, you have to swing the club *around* yourself. So the clubhead has to move *inside* the target line during your backswing and must return from inside that line if it is to travel along the line at impact. Once the clubhead moves outside the line on your downswing it becomes mechanically *impossible* for it to travel *along* that path to strike the ball. Understand — the correct clubhead path is from the inside, to along, then back *inside* the target line on your forward swing. In other words, on a normal golf swing the clubhead should never cross the target line — before, during or after impact!

And there is a second requirement for the perfectly straight shot you have in mind. At impact, your clubhead must be facing squarely in the same direction it is moving. Obviously, if your clubhead is moving down the line but your clubface is looking away from the target, you're going to strike the ball a glancing blow. If the face of the club is looking to the right, it will impart sidespin that will cause the ball to curve in that direction — "slice." If it's looking left at impact, it will apply sidespin that will cause the ball to "hook" to the left.

25

The "target line" is an imaginary line extending from the ball through the target hole. In the proper golf swing, the clubhead moves along and inside the target line (the player's side) on the backswing, then down, along and back up on the inside to the follow-through. A common mistake is to bring the clubhead down into the ball from OUTSIDE the line to INSIDE at impact.

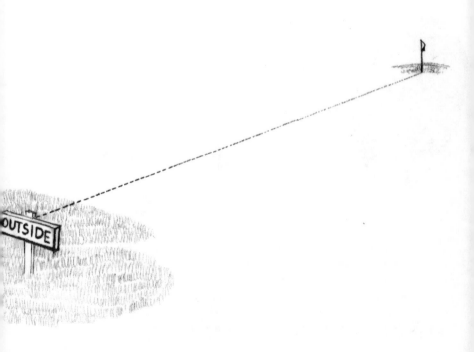

At this point you may ask, "Why can't I keep the clubface looking straight at the target throughout the swing?" The answer is obvious. You're standing alongside the target line and there is simply no way, anatomically speaking, you can keep the clubface square to the target during a full swing.

It should also be obvious that, when the clubhead reaches the bottom of the swing arc, it must be at ball level. This is your "angle of attack." If the angle of attack is too steep — if the clubhead is descending at too sharp an angle — the force of the blow will be predominantly downward rather than forward and the ball isn't going to travel very far. Conversely, if your angle of attack is too shallow, you risk stubbing the club into the ground behind the ball or catching the ball on the upswing after the clubhead has already passed the bottom of its arc.

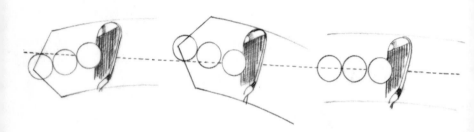

The flight of the ball is determined largely by the path of the clubhead as it moves into the ball. Here we see three impact situations with the clubhead aligned squarely with the ball in each case. But if (a) the clubhead is moving from outside-in, the path will give the ball sidespin to fly it left; if (b) from inside-out, the spin will carry the ball right. Correct path of the clubface is shown in the third drawing.

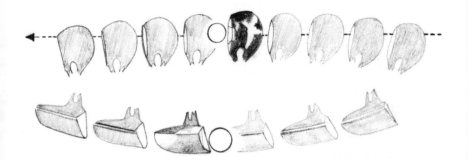

Perfect impact is shown in top drawing, with the clubhead moving into the ball along a gradually descending path, moving slightly from inside-to-along-back-to-inside. Lower drawing shows incorrect clubhead path, moving into the ball from the outside and (as is usually the case) at too steep an angle of approach. On the other hand, if the path is too sharply from the inside, the angle of attack becomes too shallow and the force of the blow is directed to the right of the target — and frequently dissipated because the clubhead will strike the turf well behind the ball.

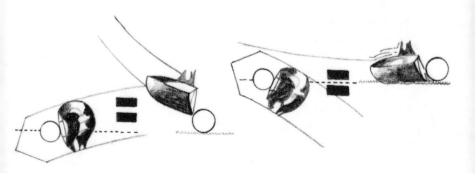

By now these things should be clear to you:
- The correct golf swing is from the inside, to along the target line, and finishing inside the line.
- The golf swing is up, down and up again.
- The clubface must turn gradually away from the target in a clockwise motion as your body turns away and your arms swing the club around and up on your backswing.
- To make a straight, solid shot, the clubhead must be moving squarely along the target line at impact, and at ball level.
- Your angle of attack must not be too steep or too shallow.

Now there's one more critical ingredient in the swing. The ball must travel the correct *distance*. Assuming you have selected the correct club for the distance, the governing factor is clubhead speed at impact. The rule is: given solid contact, the faster your clubhead moves into the ball, the farther the shot will carry with any club.

Clubhead speed comes from building as much potential energy as you can during the *backswing*, and then releasing it *fully* and *at the right instant* in the *forward swing*. Memorize that sentence because it contains the secret of the big golf hit. You have to build up energy, not waste it. Then you have to explode it, not fizzle it. You build energy with a slow, wide backswing and a full turn of the body. If you bring the club back too fast you waste energy and probably will lose control of the club.

The second reason for the slow backswing is this: the idea is to set the club in the proper position at the top of the backswing. Ideally, the shaft should parallel the target line. Imagine the shaft extended along the target line and you will have a mental picture of two parallel lines, like a railroad track.

Now you have placed the club in the proper position to return it to the ball along the target line and at the correct angle of attack. And you are in a good position to permit a full, free release of energy on the forward swing.

At this stage of your golfing career, I think you should be trying to crush your tee shots as far as you can. This will stretch your power muscles and get you in the habit of using all that power. You may not always hit the ball as solidly or as straight as you'd like, but you will develop control as you and your game mature.

Another concept you should understand before we get into the

BACKSWING

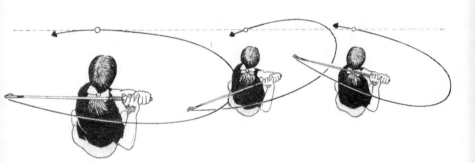

The purpose of the backswing is to set the club for the downswing. Ideally, it should set the club shaft parallel to the intended target line of the shot. Pointing it too far left (middle drawing) usually results in an outside-in swing. Pointing it right of the target line results in a "push," an inside-out swing that flies the ball to the right of the target.

fundamentals of the golf swing is what makes a golf ball go up, what makes it fly straight, and what causes it to spin sideways.

For a golf shot to fly through the air, the ball *must* have some degree of backspin. The ball rides on a cushion of air which keeps it aloft for a longer period of time. This air cushion is created by the backspin which, in turn, is due to the dimple design of the ball. Without backspin and depending entirely on the loft of the club and force of the blow, the ball will drop to earth rather quickly.

Sidespin will cause the ball to curve from left to right, or right to left, in flight. The tendency to spin sideways is greater with the less lofted clubs. Why? Because the deeper the loft on the clubface the more backspin is applied to the ball and backspin tends to offset the effect of sidespin.

There are four principles governing spin:

1. The ball will spin only when struck a glancing blow.

2. To produce a glancing blow, the clubface must be *looking away from the target* when the ball is struck.

3. Sidespin will cause the ball to curve in the direction the clubface is looking at impact.

4. The further astray the clubface is looking at impact, the greater the spin — and the wider the curve in relation to the distance traveled.

I know this is a lot to digest at one gulp, so I will give you some examples to explain these important principles.

EXAMPLE 1: At impact, the clubhead is moving *parallel* to the ground *at ball* level; the clubhead is moving *down the target line;* the clubface is *square* to this path of movement.

At first glance, it might seem these conditions would *not* cause a glancing blow and, therefore, according to Principle 1, would *not* cause spin. What you must remember is that every club in your bag, except perhaps your putter, has some degree of clubface loft. In other words, the face looks upward to some extent.

Because of this loft, in this example the clubface is looking *upward* while the clubhead is moving *forward* parallel to the ground. So the ball must spin because the blow is a glancing one (Principle 1). The blow is glancing because the clubface is looking in a different direction (upward) while the clubhead is moving forward. This is Principle 2. This spin will cause the ball to curve upward in the direction the clubface was looking, instead of forward to the direction that the

HOW SPIN AFFECTS YOUR SHOTS

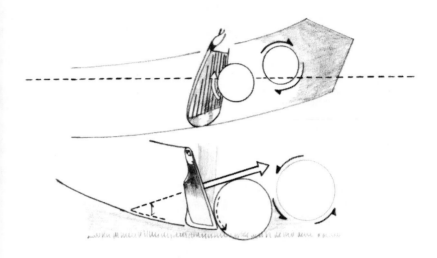

Spin is imparted by the clubface, depending on which way it is "looking" at impact. It is, by definition, a glancing blow. The first drawing shows sidespin being applied because the clubface is "looking" to the right while moving to the left. In the second drawing, we see backspin applied because the clubface is (by design) "lofted" — that is, looking up. The club is designed to apply backspin because, according to the laws of aerodynamics, backspin keeps the ball aloft for a greater distance.

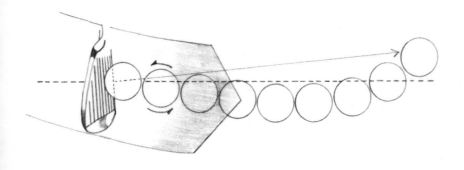

Spin tends to curve the ball in the direction the clubface is look-ing at impact and away from the direction it was moving. Here we see the clubhead looking left of the direction it is moving. The ball will eventually curve left.

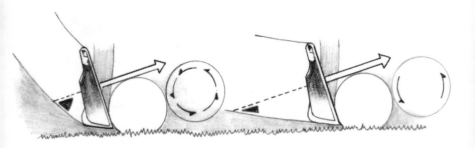

The greater the difference between the direction the clubface is looking and the path on which it is traveling at impact, the more spin will be applied. Here we see that the clubface descending at a steep angle will apply more backspin than the clubface descending at a shallower angle. Thus, the accomplished golfer will strike down for-cibly when he wants the ball to fly at a high trajectory and come to a quick halt on landing.

clubhead was moving (Principle 3). The amount it will spin upward depends, in part, on the difference between the club's upward facing and its forward movement or, in this case, on the club's degree of loft (Principle 4).

In this example, I have described a good golf shot. All good golf shots must have some degree of backspin. This causes the ball to rise and remain for a while in the air.

EXAMPLE 2: The same conditions as cited in Example 1 except that the clubhead is moving *upward* instead of *parallel* to the ground at impact.

In this case, since the clubhead is moving upward (in the same direction given the clubface by its loft), there is *less difference* between its facing and its path of movement. Therefore, because of Principle 4, this decreased difference produces *less* spin and less upward curve. This example is very important because many beginners think they must scoop upward — swing *up* to the ball — to get it into the air. As we see here, this upward path of the clubhead actually will *reduce* spin and *decrease* the height of the shot. So, never try to scoop shots. Let the club's built-in loft make the ball fly through the air.

EXAMPLE 3: Good golfers try to hit iron shots while the clubhead is moving *slightly* downward, before it reaches the bottom of its arc and starts upward. You will notice that, as a result, the good players take a divot (raise the turf) in front of the ball's original position on many iron shots. Striking the ball while the clubhead is moving slightly downward gives the ball more backspin which tends to offset any sidespin that might cause the ball to curve off line. This explains, also, why a well-struck iron shot will "bite" when it lands on the green, and often spin backward.

EXAMPLE 4: Clubhead path across the line from the *outside to the inside*. The clubface looking down the line at impact.

Here we find spin applied because the blow is a glancing one (Principle 1). The blow is glancing because the club is facing in a different direction than it is moving (Principle 2). The shot will curve right because the clubface is looking to the right of the target (Principle 3). This is a typical "slice."

By now, you should be getting familiar with the four principles of spin and how they affect golf shots. There are many other examples, but the principles remain the same.

If, for instance, your clubhead is moving from the outside to the inside but the face is looking to the left of the target, your shot will start left and then continue to spin left (in the direction the clubface is looking).

If your clubhead is moving down the target line but facing right or left of it, your shot will curve to the right or to the left respectively. If the path is inside-to-outside across the line, the ball will start out to the right and then curve either to the left, or further to the right, depending on whether the face is looking left or right of this path of movement.

These are the ballistic principles of golf. If you understand them, you will forever be able to watch your shots and recognize immediately what is causing them to fly left or right, or too high or too low.

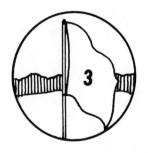

SIX FUNDAMENTALS YOU SHOULD MASTER

The six fundamentals that follow are the same ones I taught Jack Nicklaus, am now teaching Jack Nicklaus, Jr., and no doubt would teach you if we were face to face on the lesson tee. These constitute the base on which you will build your golf game.

I must tell you in all honesty, however, that learning to apply these (or any other) golf fundamentals properly and consistently requires effort. I feel it takes a novice junior golfer about five years, practicing three or four times a week, to absorb these fundamentals to the point where they become second nature.

Perhaps you're not willing to make such an all-out effort. Perhaps you will be willing to settle for whatever level of skill comes easily to you over, say, a period of a few weeks. The degree of effort you are willing to invest is up to you, of course. My only wish is that, whatever effort you do make will be devoted exclusively to these fundamentals. In that way, I feel you will be getting the greatest return on your investment of time and energy.

FUNDAMENTAL 1: Set Up Correctly

It was the 1974 U.S. Open at Winged Foot in Mamaroneck, New York, and I was watching Nicklaus warm up on the practice range. I couldn't recall ever seeing him swing so badly.

Jack didn't realize it but he was obviously setting up to his shots (addressing the ball) with an extremely "closed" shoulder alignment. By this I mean his upper body was aligned so, if you laid a club across his chest, the shaft would point far to the right of his target.

Now, the last thing you want to do to a friend is to start him thinking about changing his swing a few minutes before he's going to tee it up in the Open Championship. However, Jack's alignment was so bad it was forcing him to make a screwball swing in order to get his shots anywhere near his target. I figured I couldn't put him in any worse shape than he already was.

So I asked him, "Jack, where are you aiming?"

"At that tree," he answered, pointing down the center of the range.

"See that fence over there on the right?" I asked. "Well, as far as I'm concerned that is 'out of bounds' — and you're aiming your shoulders to the *right* of that fence."

Proper alignment is an important factor. Even the professional players frequently ask a colleague to check their alignment because they tend to fall into bad habits. One way to check your alignment is to lay a club along the ground pointing at a given target, then check your address position with reference to this line. You will be surprised at how easily you can drift into error.

I guess he decided he didn't want to change things at that time, but a few days later we were standing on the sixth tee of the Memorial Course he built at Muirfield Village in Columbus, Ohio. He was still aligning his shoulders far to the right. I went up and grabbed his shoulders, turned them around so they were slightly 'open' — aligned slightly *left* of the center of the fairway. The new alignment felt terrible to Jack as I knew it would.

"I can't hit it from here," he said. "I'll go 'way back over there to the left."

"Then just let it go over there," I told him.

With that he swung and hit the ball . . . bam! . . . right down the middle of the fairway. Then he hit some more drives with his new shoulder alignment. One after another, they split the fairway.

I know Jack won't mind me mentioning this incident because it makes the point that setting up correctly is all-important — and it's easy for even the world's best golfer to fall into a bad set-up pattern. I want to emphasize that nothing has more to do with the success or failure of your shots than the way you position your club and yourself before you swing.

Learning to set up correctly isn't very exciting. Perhaps that's why so few golfers have good set-ups. Yet this is a basic fundamental. With a good set-up, everything else will fall into place much more readily. And without a good set-up the odds against you ever becoming a good golfer are astronomical.

Good golfers set the clubhead behind the ball and aim it on target before they adjust their feet and body in position. This makes sense because it's easier to aim your clubhead correctly than it is to aim yourself without the clubhead for a reference point.

Aiming the club is something that requires periodic checking. As even Nicklaus finds, it's so easy to start aiming right or left. When you practice, try to find someone who will stand behind you, looking down your target line, to check your aim.

Or, lay another club on the ground a few feet in front of the ball, pointing down the target line, then aim the clubface down the line formed by the club shaft. As you do so, also check your target and notice how your clubface looks, or seems to look, in relation to it. By doing this you will come to recognize how your clubface should appear to you when it is, in fact, aimed squarely at the target.

In time, you will find it easier to move directly into a correct ad-

Building A Proper Set-Up

Step 1 — Take your 5-iron, a ball and a yardstick (for precise measuring). Place the ball in front of a full-length mirror and select a target line from the mirror to some object reflected in the mirror.

Step 2 — Take your position at the ball, facing down the target line. The sole of your club should square with your target line.

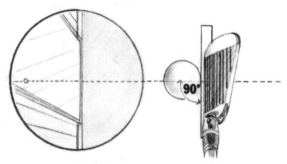

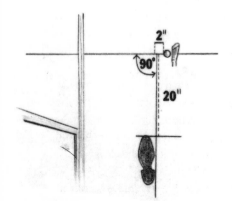

Step 3 — Place your left toe 20 inches from the target line so an imaginary line running along the inside edge of your left shoe will intersect the target line at 90 degrees and at a point two inches left of the ball.

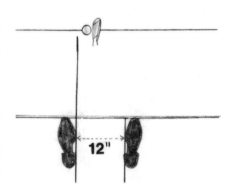

Step 4 — Place your right foot in position so it aligns with your left foot at an equal distance (20") from the target line. A line across your toes should run parallel to the target line. This is a "square" address. "Open" and "closed" stances are shown in the drawing.

12"

Step 5 — Swivel your left heel two inches to the right and your right heel one inch to the left. Now practice stepping back and then re-entering this stance until it becomes a familiar habit.

Step 6 — With your feet positioned correctly, stand perfectly upright with the club extended horizontally at arms' length.

Step 7 — Bending only from the hips, lower the clubhead into position behind the ball.

Step 8 — Flex your knees slightly by lowering your buttocks until a line across your knees will parallel your toe line about two inches on your side of it.

Building A Proper Set-Up

Step 9 — Distribute your weight more or less equally between your feet and between the ball and the heel of each foot.

Step 10 — Align your hips and chest so lines across each would run parallel to the target line, toe line and knee line. This is known as a "square" alignment. Smaller figure on the left shows variations in alignment, with toe line square, hip line open and shoulder line closed.

Step 11 — Face the mirror and check your overall stance with the figure shown here. Note the left side is somewhat lower than the right because the golfer's left hand is lower on the club shaft. Hands should be slightly forward of the clubhead; the head slightly behind the ball.

45

dress position almost subconsciously. You'll learn to find the right set-up by "feel." For the present, however, take your time and be very specific in following this procedure:

1. Check yourself in a mirror, by placing a ball on the floor and selecting a "target line" running from the ball to some object in the mirror.

2. Hold the club in both hands and place the clubhead behind the ball so it faces squarely down your target line. As you look down at it, the forward edge of the clubhead — the bottom edge of the club-face — should square off with the target line itself.

3. Place your left foot in position so (a) a line running along its inside edge would intersect at 90° ("square") angle with your target line, at (b) a point two inches to the left of the ball, and (c) so your big toe is 20 inches from your target line.

4. Place your right foot in position so (a) it sets parallel to your left foot, (b) there is a 12-inch space between your feet, and (c) a line touching the toes of each shoe runs parallel to your target line. This is what we call a "square" stance. It is "open" if your toe-line, when extended forward to the mirror, would point away from your target line, and "closed" if it would eventually cross it.

5. Swivel your left heel two inches to the right, toward your right heel. Swivel your right heel one inch to the left.

Now study the position of your feet and try to memorize how it looks in relation to the ball and your clubhead. Then step back from the ball and return to your stance. See how closely you come to the proper placement of your feet. Continue this drill until it becomes quite natural for you to place your clubhead in its proper position behind the ball, step into the correct position with your left foot and adjust your right foot accurately. This is a routine you should follow on the course as long as you play golf.

6. Having stepped into the foot position as described, but this time *not* placing your clubhead behind the ball, stand perfectly upright with the club in both hands and extended horizontally at arm's length in front of you.

7. Bending *only from the hips,* not from your upper back or neck, lower the clubhead into position behind the ball.

8. Flex your knees slightly by simply lowering your buttocks, as if starting to sit down, until a line across the tips of your knees would

Building A Proper Set-Up

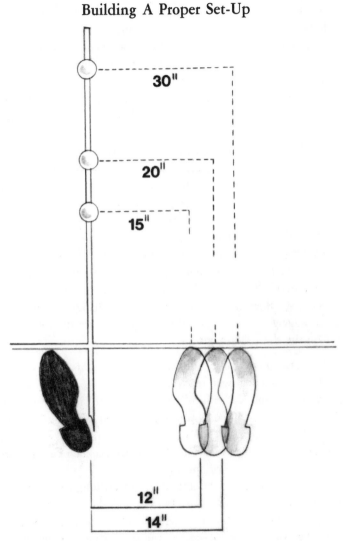

The ideal width of the stance varies from club to club depending on its length. For most players, the distance should not exceed 14 inches nor the distance from the ball to the toe line 30 inches. For the 5-iron, a medium length club, the distance from toe to ball decreases to about 20 inches, then down to 15 inches for the full wedge shot. Maximum stance for the 5-iron is 12 inches and gradually diminishes for the shorter irons.

parallel a line across your toes, and run about two inches inside it.

9. Distribute your weight more or less equally between your feet and between the ball and heel of each foot.

10. Align your hips and chest so a line across each will run parallel to your target line, your toe line·and your knee line. Once you have all these lines running parallel, you have set up "square" over-all. If any of these lines should extend away from or across your target line, that part of your set-up must be considered "open" or "closed" respectively.

11. Slide your hands and the top of the clubshaft left or right — toward or away from your target — until your left arm and your club-shaft form a fairly straight line from your left shoulder to the ball. (Important: you may raise or lower your left shoulder and side as you slide your hands left or right, but be sure not to open or close your body alignment as you do so.)

At this point, you should be set up correctly for making a proper golf swing. Make sure that your head and neck haven't slumped forward, and that your back is still straight. You will also notice that your right side, shoulder and hip, is slightly lower than your left. This is normal, largely because your right hand (if you are right-handed) is lower on the shaft than your left.

Of course, no two golfers are exactly alike in build or type of swing. So, a golf professional who teaches you face to face, may prescribe a slight variation from the set-up I've outlined. Heed his advice because he has the advantage of seeing your physique and swing pattern at first hand. However, in the absence of professional instruction, I believe the procedures I've outlined here will serve to give you a far better address position than you would adopt otherwise.

Finally, let me stress the importance of learning to set-up to the ball smoothly and without delay. In time, you should be able to step quickly into a correct position, waggle the club, and get on with your swing. The longer you stand over the ball and the more things you consciously flash through your head, the less chance you have of making a smooth, rhythmic swing.

FUNDAMENTAL 2: A Proper Grip

There are three specific requirements of a good grip.

The first is that you hold the club with just enough pressure to control it throughout the swing, including the moment of impact, but never so tightly as to inhibit a free swing. Most golfers either grip too tightly from the moment they first address the ball, or they grab hold of the club tightly, usually with their "throwing" hand, some time before impact.

Your grip pressure will change automatically in some degree as you swing, especially in that it must increase gradually as the clubhead picks up speed. However, this change should be subtle, gradual and unconscious. Sudden grabbing inhibits free swinging of the arms, free hinging and unhinging of the wrists and, in consequence, free squaring of the clubface through impact. As you swing, add only enough pressure to keep the club from slipping in your hands.

The second requirement of a good grip is that it allows your hands to work together as a unit instead of as two opposing forces. For your hands to work together, they must (a) join each other snugly, (b) take up as little space on the club as possible and (c) align together with the palms more or less facing each other.

There are three basic types of grip that join the hands together on the club. They have one thing in common: in all three grips, the thumb of the left hand rests in the palm of the right. Otherwise the relationship of the fingers differs.

In the so-called "10-finger" grip, the left forefinger and the little finger of the right hand curl around the grip side by side. The grip gets its name from the fact that all ten fingers are on the club shaft. It is probably the least popular of the three grip styles.

The so-called "interlock" grip entwines the little finger of the right hand between the forefinger and middle finger of the left. This is the grip used and advocated by Jack Nicklaus and is specifically recommended for players with small hands who appreciate the snug linking of the hands. Some fine players have used this grip including Gene Sarazen, Henry Picard, Lloyd Mangrum and John Mahaffey.

By far the most popular grip is the so-called "Vardon" grip, or overlapping grip. In this grip, the little finger of the right hand laps over the forefinger of the left hand and lies in the furrow between that

First Requirement For A Good Grip

Proper pressure is important in the grip. It's necessary for club control and free swinging. Too little pressure leads to slippage, followed immediately by clenching. The tendency of the beginner is to grip the club too tensely. Start with just enough pressure to lift the clubhead off the turf. As you swing, the weight of the moving clubhead will make you increase your finger pressure instinctively.

finger and the left middle finger. Probably 90% of the players employ this grip.

The importance of a good grip is borne out by the fact that the direction of your clubface at impact is largely determined by the direction your hands face after completing their grip. You will find that, generally speaking, the more your right palm faces *downward* at address, the more your clubface will be looking to the *right* of your target. Conversely, the more your right palm faces *upward* at address, the more likely your clubface will be looking to the *left* of your target at impact. Thus, the set of your hands at address can have a critical influence on the curving action of your shot.

I find that young players frequently try to copy the grips of experts. This places the palms more or less parallel with the clubface and faces the back of the left hand and the palm of the right hand directly forward rather than upward or downward. While this positioning is ideal for some adults, until you develop a little more golfing muscle, it may not give you enough left-hand control of the club as you swing.

If you find you either let go of the club at the top of your backswing or slice your shots from left to right, you should set your hands on the club when gripping so they are both turned slightly farther to your right. In other words, your right palm and the back of your left hand should face slightly *upward*. As you get older and stronger, or if you start hooking shots to the left, you can gradually set your hands farther to the left.

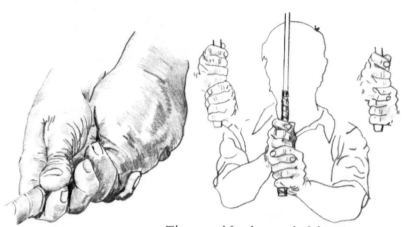

The second fundamental of the grip governs the synchronized action of the two hands. This is accomplished three ways. As shown, first, the left thumb snuggles between the thumb and heel pad of the right hand. Next, the hands are linked in any one of the three grips shown — the Overlapping (or Vardon) Grip, in which the little finger of the right hand laps over and between the left index and middle fingers; or Interlocking Grip which actually hooks the right little finger and left index finger; or the 10-Finger (or so-called "baseball") Grip. The hands should take up as little space as possible on the club shaft and the two palms should more or less face each other.

Second Grip Requirement

Third Grip Requirement

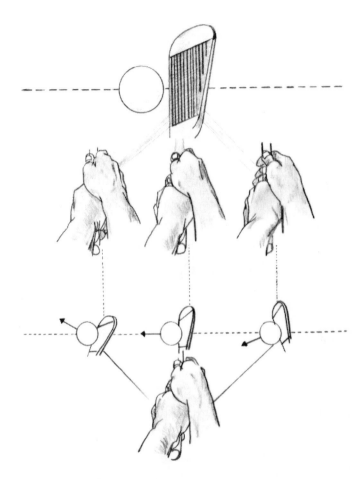

The third fundamental of the grip is to position the hands so they will return the clubface squarely to a hitting position at impact. If the left hand is positioned too far beneath the shaft the club will be returned in an "open" position with a resulting slice. Conversely, if the left hand is turned too far over the shaft with the right hand sliding under it, the result is a "closed" clubface at impact and a disastrous hook shot. The correct hand position (uncomfortable until you get accustomed to it) is a "squeezing" effect of the two hands with the two V's between the thumb and forefinger pointing to their respective shoulders.

FUNDAMENTAL 3: Steady Head

Your head is the hub or axis of your swing, around which you turn your torso and swing your club.

Ideally, you should position your head slightly behind the ball as you set up to your shot. Put your left cheek about even with the back of the ball. Next, just before you start your backswing, turn your chin an inch or two toward your right shoulder. Finally, hold that head position until *after* you have hit the ball when the momentum of your swing will force you to rotate your chin to your left.

Simple? It wasn't for Jack Nicklaus.

Turning your head to your right and then keeping it steady — not rigid — until after impact causes many good things to happen in your golf swing:

- It helps you start the club back slowly and smoothly.
- It clears the way for your shoulders to turn fully and freely on your backswing.
- It helps produce a full, springlike coiling of your muscles on the backswing for greater build-up of potential clubhead speed.
- It prevents sideways or up-down swaying that might distort your swing path and arc, or inhibit full coiling.
- It sets and keeps your eyes in position for you to "see" the proper path along which your clubhead should approach the ball (from inside to along the target line).

I doubt you will ever reach the point where your head doesn't shift slightly at some point during most of your swings. Studies of touring professionals show some slight head movement even in their case — usually slightly down and away from the target on the forward swing. The message I want to leave with you, however, is that even though you may never achieve perfection with this particular fundamental, the closer you come to it as you develop your golf game, the better you will play the rest of your life.

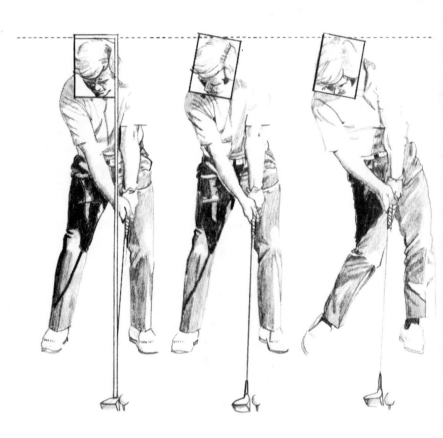

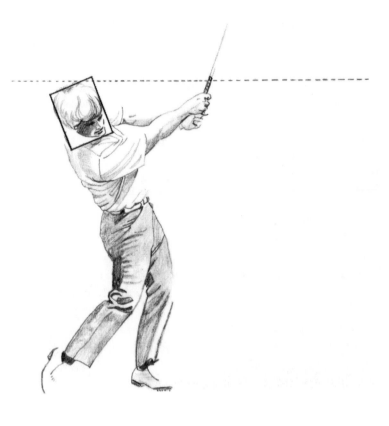

The ideal head position, as illustrated, helps you maintain body balance while you swing and block any horizontal or vertical swaying. Addressing the ball with your head slightly behind the ball, then cocking your chin to the right starting your backswing, maintain this chin cock through impact and, finally, lets it turn to the target as your shoulders turn through.

FUNDAMENTAL 4: Proper Footwork

Proper footwork is simply a matter of rolling your ankles correctly while keeping your knees flexed at all times. On the backswing, your left ankle rolls inward toward your right foot so that most of your weight shifts from left to right onto the *inside* of the right foot (the rest remaining on the inside of the left). Then, at the start of the downswing, *both* ankles roll laterally to the left so your weight gradually shifts from the inside of your right foot to the inside of your left foot.

This simple to-and-fro working of the ankles will give supple golfers all the body motion they need while swinging. In fact, I teach a drill to junior golfers in which they never lift the left heel during the backswing. This deepens their sense of balance and forces them to develop a full arm swing. To provide a full body turn, older and less supple golfers may need to allow the left heel to lift slightly as they roll the ankle to the inside during the backswing. As far as the right heel is concerned, it should lift gradually as your arms swing forward and upward after impact. Basically, however, proper footwork is merely a matter of rolling the ankles as I've described.

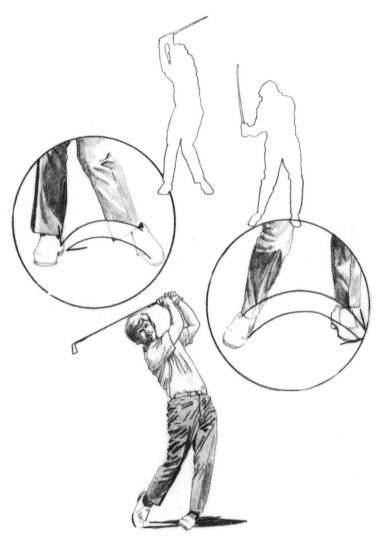

Proper footwork is mostly a matter of rolling the ankles so the body weight shifts to and from the insides of the feet. On the backswing, the left ankle rolls to the right so most of your weight feels like it has shifted to the inside of your right foot. At the start of downswing, the right ankle rolls to the left, shifting the weight onto your left foot. This shift continues through the swing until it finishes with almost all your weight on your left foot.

59

FUNDAMENTAL 5: Full Extension

Full extension is a matter of using all your physical self as you swing — of fully stretching and coiling all the muscles of your body that need stretching and coiling. Most of that stretching and coiling is done during your backswing, to allow for later unstretching and uncoiling as you return the club to the ball.

Full extension is simple to explain, but physically demanding to execute. It involves three things during your backswing:

1. Making as full a turning of the hips as you possibly can short of straightening your right leg or shifting your weight onto the outside of your right foot.

2. Making as full a shoulder turn as you can while keeping your head steady.

3. Swinging your hands on as wide and as high an arc as you can short of shifting your head position or loosening your hold on the club.

Full extension on the backswing is the key to getting maximum distance from your shots. This requires (1) a full hip turn without straightening your right leg or shifting your weight to the OUTSIDE of the right foot, then (2) make as full a shoulder turn as you can without moving your head, and, finally (3) swing your hands as wide and high as you can without shifting your head or loosening your grip.

FUNDAMENTAL 6: Quiet Hands

I suppose it is only natural that we rely on our hands and wrists in golf, just as we use them for so many different functions in everyday living. I also suppose it is only natural that we tend to over-use our hands and wrists at the very start of our downswing, because at this time our eagerness or anxiety about striking the ball is most likely to overwhelm us.

Too much wristiness at the start of the downswing can ruin an otherwise superior golf swing because flashing the club down with the hands can (a) throw the clubhead off path, (b) misalign the clubface, (c) waste clubhead speed before impact, or (d) cause any combination of these errors.

Once you develop your footwork as described in Fundamental 4, the first move of the downswing will take place automatically *if you let it happen.* While I don't believe there should be an actual pause at the top of the backswing, I do feel most golfers should *feel* a momentary "waiting" at the top, a waiting with the hands and shoulders for the feet to shift some weight toward the target.

It is important also to remember to *swing* the club. That may sound ridiculously elementary but too many golfers, trying to use their legs correctly, forget that it is the clubhead which strikes the ball. Yes, the feet start the downswing, but the arms — not the hands — must do their part to swing the club down and "through" the ball.

As long as your feet work correctly and lead your downswing, on all your shots you should try to accelerate your arms (and thus the club) through the impact zone as fast as you possibly can without losing your balance. Do this and your hands will react automatically to the weight and speed of the moving clubhead. Your wrists will uncock automatically to square the clubface at the proper moment, as long as you also shift your weight and keep a steady head. You'll risk big trouble, however, if you consciously attempt to apply your hands and wrists to the shot.

You youngsters, at this stage of your lives, have a God-given knack for imitation. Use this knack by watching good golfers swing. As you do, keep in mind the six fundamentals I've described in this chapter. Watch how the experts apply them and the rhythm with which they apply them. The more you watch others act out the basics I've described, the easier it will be for you to master them yourself.

Beware of flipping your hands and wrists too early on the downswing. Maintain the cocked wrists until you near the impact position. The drawings show an increasing distance between the hands and shoulder. This indicates free arm-swinging as opposed to shoulder shoving. The angle formed by the left arm and clubshaft, indicating the degree of wrist cock, remains intact.

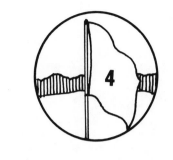

SAVING SHOTS

In golf, they don't ask *how*. They just ask: *How many?* The score is everything. So, when your drive winds up behind a tree, or when you miss the green and the ball buries in sand, your immediate job is to cut your losses — to save strokes — so you can go onto the next hole with some chance of still winning the war.

In this chapter I will tell you how to plan and play the shots you will need most frequently when the battle goes against you. You will find, too, that these same stroke-saving shots, played to minimize your losses, sometimes will actually turn the tide of battle, or even the war. Many a match that seemed hopelessly lost has been won with a single well-played "trouble" shot by a struggling golfer who refused to wave the white flag.

Club Selection

Every club in your bag is designed to hit shots a different distance. The trick in club selection, therefore, is (a) to know your normal distance with each club, (b) the length of the shot at hand, and (c) to match the two successfully.

The simplest way to determine how far you hit the ball with each club is to pace off the length of your shots. But first you must learn to take steps one yard in length. You can develop this skill quickly by merely taking a yardstick, measuring off five yards of turf or flooring, and pacing the distance in five equal steps.

After that, make it a habit to pace off the length of your good shots with various clubs, but only when the ball has carried and rolled an average distance. Over a period of time, you will acquire a fairly precise knowledge of which club you should select and how hard to swing it to make a shot of, say, 143 yards, or 167 yards, or 110 yards. Of course, you won't hit your shots precisely the correct distance every time, or even most of the time. But you *will* come closer more frequently as you sharpen your sense of distance and understanding of each club's potential.

Once you know a hole's playing distance, it becomes relatively easy to determine how far your approach shot must travel to reach the green. You merely subtract the total length of the shot you've just played from the hole's overall playing length.

Today most courses are measured fairly reliably, but you will find some that give misleading yardages on the scorecard. Such badly

The thinking golfer establishes his own yardstick. He knows, almost to the yard, how far he normally hits each club in his bag. After that, it's simple mathematics in making his club selection. A golf hole is measured from the center of the tee to the center of the green, following a line of play intended by the architect. Shifting of the tee markers and the hole can make a 20-yard difference in the play of the hole — and wind and rain-softened turf can effect the flight and run of the ball.

measured courses will become apparent to you after only a few holes. Then you will have to fall back on your sense of depth perception and your observation of the approach shots of others in your group. When in doubt about which of two clubs to use, observe the hazards around the green. You'll probably want to use the longer club if the major trouble is in front of the green, or a shorter club if the danger lies behind it.

Shot Visualization

Apart from applying the fundamentals of the previous chapter and selecting the right club, there is one other important stroke-saving aid that you should apply on *every* shot you ever play. That one thing is to visualize the intended shot *before* you play it. Picture the shot in your mind's eye. See it fly through the air and bounce and roll to the hole. It's a confidence-builder. Similarly, when you reach the green, visualize your putt rolling forward, perhaps following the slope of the green, then nose-diving into the cup.

The reason for this pre-shot visualization is to give your mind and body a definite and positive course of action. Visualizing the shot before you swing is like visualizing a house you've visited many times before. By visualizing it before you return to it, you can then drive to it quickly and directly, without hesitation. By visualizing the golf shot beforehand, you tell your mind and muscles exactly what you want them to accomplish. This encourages them to respond accordingly by providing them with a clear objective.

Hilly Lies

Inevitably, there will be times when your ball doesn't finish on level ground. You will save yourself some strokes if you know beforehand how the ball reacts when struck from various types of angled lies.

When you're dealing with a SIDEHILLER (the ball lying either above or below your feet), you can expect the ball to fly *away from the slope of the hill*. Thus, if you're standing *below* the ball, you can expect the ball to *pull to the left* of the target line, away from the hillside. So, aim to the right of your target. Conversely, when you're standing *above* the ball, you can expect it to *push right*. So you should aim to the left.

On downhill shots (when your target line slopes downward) you can expect the ball to *push right*. Uphill lies will *pull left*. Aim your

Hilly lies require special adjustments to maintain balance and allow for the probable flight of the ball. A downhill lie (a) will tend to push to the right. Grip the club shaft at its extreme length and aim yourself and the clubface to the left of the target. An uphill lie (b) calls for opposite treatment, "choking" down on the shaft and aiming right of the target to anticipate a probable pulled shot. On uphill shots (c) plant your right foot and set your body vertical to the slope; play the ball forward off your front foot. On downhill shots (d) reverse this procedure.

shots accordingly.

On hilly lies it's important to maintain your balance when you swing. The natural tendency is to fall away on the downhill slope. Thus, you have to set your weight more toward your uphill foot to brace yourself against this tendency. For the same reason, on sidehill lies, you must set your weight more than normally toward your toes or heels, whichever are higher on the hill.

The only other thing you must do with hilly lies is to position yourself properly to make solid contact with the ball. On uphill and downhill lies this means tilting yourself to the right or left so your body sets more or less perpendicular to the slope. This positions you to swing the clubhead *along* the line of slope instead of *into* it. You'll also find that, on downhill lies, you will make much better contact if you play the ball a bit more toward your high foot.

On sidehill lies when the ball is above your feet (and closer than normal to your hands), you should choke down on the club to avoid undercutting the ball. When it's below your feet (and farther from your hands) you'll need to grip the club at the end of the shaft and stand a bit closer to the ball than usual to avoid topping.

Shots From the Rough

Your first thought on shots from long grass should be to play your *next* shot from short grass. In other words, get out of the rough and back in play!

The next most important thought in the rough is choosing the right club. The temptation is to select a long iron — with relatively little loft — to recover as much lost distance as possible. Unless the ball is sitting up cleanly in a good open lie, this can be a disastrous decision. Too often, these clubs lack the loft to get the ball up and on its way out of the deep surrounding grass.

When in doubt between two clubs on a shot from deep rough, always go with the one having the most loft. The ball will come out cleaner and higher and will carry farther, meaning you'll lose very little distance and you'll be in much better position for further recovery.

The higher lofted wood clubs — the 4, 5 and 6 woods — are handy weapons to use from fairly good lies when the grass isn't too deep or thick. The beveled, wider bottoms of their heads tend to pancake the grass and slide over it. Thus they encounter less resistance and are less apt to get tangled in the long grass than the thin-bladed irons.

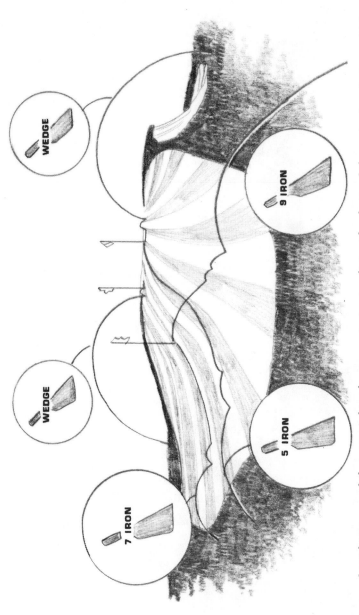

Chipping and pitching around the green is largely an exercise in visualizing the shot and then selecting the iron which will permit you to attack the shot with the greatest confidence. Plan your shots to bounce and roll to the hole whenever possible. The drawing shows a variety of situations you will encounter and the ideal way to play each shot.

The chip shot (upper drawing) is a low flying, running shot played with a less lofted club and a shallow swing, back and through. The pitch shot (below) follows a higher trajectory and settles quickly on landing. It calls for a steeper swing angle with more wrist cocking and uncocking.. In both cases, however, your hands must lead the clubhead through the shot so that impact is made before the clubhead reaches the bottom of its arc. Beware of trying to "scoop" the ball. This is a deadly sin.

"Part Shots" — Chipping and Pitching

There will be times when a full shot with even a 9-iron or wedge will overshoot your target. Then you need to know how to play "part shots" — strokes made with less than a full swing. There are two basic types of part shots: chip shots and pitch shots. When you play them you are either "chipping" or "pitching."

The main difference between a chip shot and a pitch shot is its trajectory. Your basic chip shot features minimum "carry" and maximum roll, ideally landing on the green and bouncing and rolling the rest of the way to the hole. The pitch shot features maximum carry and minimum roll, landing close to the hole and then, hopefully, stopping with little additional forward movement.

Both of these part shots are essential to every golfer's shotmaking arsenal. The higher pitch shot is usually the more risky of the two in that it must be played with a highly-lofted club — wedge or 9-iron — in order to make the ball fly higher and settle quickly. Thus, it takes a longer swing to pitch the ball the same distance you could chip it with a less lofted club. The longer swing, for most golfers, increases the risk of mishitting the ball.

You'll be a far better chipper and pitcher if you bear in mind:

1. Always visualize how you *think* the shot should look before playing it.

2. Visualize a part shot landing on the green whenever conditions permit because the surface is smoother and more consistent than the fairway.

3. Visualize a part shot landing on a level area of the green whenever possible.

4. Whenever possible, visualize a chip shot rather than a pitch shot. "See" the ball landing five or six feet onto the green, then rolling to the hole. Pitch the ball to the hole only when running the chip shot would most likely cause the ball to roll well past the cup, or when chipping would require you to land the ball on a downslope.

5. Choose the club which will most easily give you the shot you've visualized.

6. Take one or more practice swings until you find the stroke you will need to produce the shot you have in mind with the club you've selected.

7. Duplicate the stroke you've just rehearsed as you make the actual shot.

When practicing chipping and pitching, here are some basic techniques:

a. The shorter the shot, the more you should choke down on the club, narrow your stance, and stand closer to the ball. In effect, give yourself maximum control of the clubhead by gripping the shaft closer to the clubhead, but don't actually move your hands down onto the metal shaft.

b. Try to catch the ball at the bottom, or *just before the bottom,* of your swing arc. Strike it with a *downward*-forward action of the clubhead, never with an *upward*-forward scoop. On chip shots use a shallower swing arc — more forward than downward. On pitch shots, use a steeper arc — more downward than forward. These different arcs make your chip shots run forward and your pitch shots pop upward.

c. Make sure your left hand leads, not follows, your clubhead. This helps assure that the clubhead moves downward, not upward, to the ball.

d. Make sure your forearms accelerate, not decelerate, to avoid flipping the clubhead upward with your wrists.

e. Keep that head steady!

Sand Shots

The first thing you need to play these shots is a sand wedge, a club specially designed for bunker play. It has a heavy head to cut under the ball and through the sand and a thick flange that tends to "bounce" the club out of the sand after lifting the ball out of its lie instead of burying itself in the sand. If you hold the head of the sand wedge at eye level you will notice that its bottom, or sole is unlike your other irons in that the leading edge of the sole is actually higher than its trailing edge.

The lower back edge of the sole is called the "bounce" and acts as a rudder to keep the club head from cutting too deeply or burying itself in the sand. Once you learn to use the bounce on your sand wedge, bunker play will hold no fears for you. In fact, you will enjoy playing the shot.

You can control the depth of your cut in the sand by opening or closing the clubface. The more you open the face to the right, the more bounce effect you will get as you swing through the sand and the shallower will be your slice of sand. The more you close the face, the more you'll use the leading edge and the deeper will be the penetra-

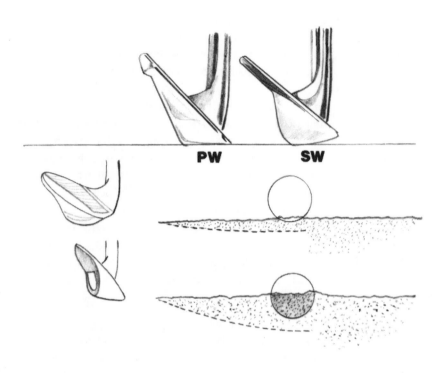

PW   SW

THE SAND SHOT

*The principle underlying the sand shot is to slide the clubhead under
the ball, lifting it out of the bunker on a cushion of sand. The sand
wedge, with its heavily weighted sole and lower trailing edge of the
blade, is specially designed for the job. The more you "open" the blade
the shallower will be the "sand divot" and, conversely, closing the blade
will result in a deeper bite in the sand. The secret of the successful sand
shot is an early cocking of the wrist on the take-away, a steep angle
of attack, and a full follow-through. After that, it's mostly a matter
of staying down to the shot and training yourself to take a 10-to-12-inch
slice of sand on which the ball will ride out of the bunker.*

tion of the club in the sand.

So, the deeper your ball sits in the sand, the less you will want to open your clubface at address. When most of the ball lies lower than the surrounding surface of the sand, you'll want to close the clubface to the left of the target, actually. Remember, the idea is to cut *under* the ball without cutting so deeply that your clubhead can't pass through the sand.

Naturally, you'll find that the ball flies and rolls to the left of your target when you close the clubface in that direction, and to the right when you open it to the right. To counteract this misdirection, you must align yourself — and especially your shoulders — more to the right of your target when you close the clubface and to the left when opening it.

While clubface alignment controls the depth of your sand "divot" to a large degree, your angle of attack also has an effect. In bunkers you want to attack the ball from a rather steep angle to be sure and cut *under* the ball and not just slap the surface of the sand like a stone skipping on the surface of the water. There is danger then of the clubhead bouncing up into the ball's back side. To give your swing this steepness, use an early wrist cock on the backswing to get the clubhead moving abruptly upward. Then apply a strong downward pulling action with your left hand and arm on the downswing.

Finally, use your legs as much as you can during your forward swing. Dig your feet into the sand at address and then work your ankles as best you can. The more you can use your legs on your forward swing, the longer the slice of sand you will take. The longer the slice you take, the farther behind the ball you can safely enter the sand without fear of bouncing the clubhead into the ball. With practice, you will be able to take at least a 12-inch sand "divot" and thus cut into the sand a good four or five inches behind the ball. This all but eliminates the so-called "thin" shot which catches the ball cleanly and airmails it over the green.

Above all, remember that sand traps are *hazards*. That means you cannot ground your clubhead or otherwise touch the sand with your club until you swing it forward during your actual stroke. The penalty for this breach of the rules is two strokes in stroke play or loss of the hole in match play.

Putting

Putting is the ultimate stroke saver. And since the object of the game is to take the fewest possible strokes, doesn't it make sense to spend a lot of time in putting practice? Very few golfers really practice this critically important phase of the game. They prefer to bang away with the heavy artillery on the driving range. But those golfers who play the game for their living spend more time on their putting than on any other type of shot.

Good putting is largely a matter of confidence, planning, sensitivity and sound technique. All of these ingredients are important, but if I had to settle for a full measure of only one, I'd certainly choose "confidence." If you *know* you're going to hole a certain putt, you can all but stand on your head and strike it and the ball will find the cup.

Unfortunately, confidence isn't something you can buy at the golf shop. It comes, in part, from knowing you've planned the putt correctly — that you've "read" the green accurately — and you're satisfied that your hands can produce the putt you've planned.

Planning a putt involves reading the character of the terrain and grass between your ball and the cup. It means sensing just how fast the ball must run, in which direction and in what degree it will "break," or curve off-line in order to finish its run in the hole. The confident putter, again, will "see" the ball actually tracking into the cup.

There are several different ways to sink a given putt. Let's say you have a 5-foot sidehiller that obviously is going to curve from left to right. The degree of this "break" will depend largely on how firmly you strike the ball since the degree of curvature will increase as the ball decelerates. Thus, you can tap it gently and let it curve as much as six to ten inches. Or you can ram it firmly and expect only an inch or two of break. Consequently, every putt requires two decisions — how firmly to strike it and where to aim it.

Once you've made these two decisions, you should carry this image in your mind's eye until you've actually started the putt on its way.

There are many tricks to reading greens correctly. For the moment, however, here are a few observations you might want to tuck away in your memory bank:

1. The faster the ball will roll on a given surface, the less it will curve sideways.

2. The ball will always roll faster immediately after leaving the blade and will be more likely to curve as it slows down approaching the hole.

3. Most greens slant downward to some degree from back to front.

4. Sidehill putts are more likely to curve more on greens with grass

"On The Lesson Tee"

Putting is largely a matter of confidence and "feel." The good putter establishes in his mind's eye the likely line which will carry the ball into the hole, strokes the ball with what he has determined to be the proper speed, and visualizes its journey all the way to the hole.

that is dry, or cut short, or is sparse and thin-bladed, especially when the putt is moving slowly.

5. You can expect less sidehill break on greens with grass that is wet, or cut long and growing, or is thick or thick-bladed.

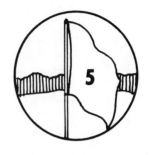

GETTING BETTER

Progress in golf comes in peaks and valleys. One day you'll peak and shoot a "career" round. The next day, or the day after, you'll play about as dismal a round as you could ever imagine. That's why the Scottish philosopher described it as an 'umblin' game. The thrill of victory and the agony of defeat go hand-in-hand . . . and that's what makes golf the exasperating and fascinating game that it is.

On bad days, it's best to remember what I said about peaks and valleys. Just continue to work on the fundamentals and your stroke-saving shots and, in time, you will come gradually to recognize that your peaks are getting higher and more frequent and your valleys are beginning to fill in.

The second thing to bear in mind about progress is that sometimes you will play your *worst* after you've been practicing and working hard on something new. Our bodies are slaves to habit. They resist new positions and new movements. Change is foreign and often uncomfortable. This discomfort usually is temporary, but it can definitely cause you to hit bad shots and shoot high scores until the new changes begin to feel natural.

The point is: Don't give up on a sound fundamental just because it doesn't work at first. You probably have been "grooving" your mistakes for a long time. It will take considerable effort to rechannel your swing until it feels natural and comfortable. What I'm saying is, don't let a few bad shots turn you away from mastering a valid fundamental.

A third discouraging thing that frustrates a majority of golfers as they try to improve is the difficulty they encounter when they try to take their newfound skills from the practice tee to the golf course. Nothing is more likely to fill the learning golfer with a sense of frustration and aggravation than to hit shot after shot perfectly on the range, then dub one after another when he tries to translate his new mastery into a lower score.

When this happens just remember these *facts*:

• On the practice tee you hit shot after shot with the same club. On the golf course you rarely use the same club twice in a row.

• On the practice tee you hit shot after shot in rapid succession. On the golf course, the wait between shots allows the muscles to tighten and your sense of rhythm to dull.

• On the practice tee you're hitting all shots from a level lie. On the course you're frequently hitting from angled lies.

• On the practice tee you aren't worried about incurring a penalty for hitting a shot off-line. On the golf course this subtle pressure is always present.

• On the practice tee bad shots cost you nothing but waste motion. On the course they could cost you the battle, even the war.

All of these factors contribute to making the game much more difficult than the practice. By understanding this, I hope you'll keep forging ahead with your improvement program even when the going seems all uphill and very discouraging.

Taking Lessons

As golfers, we may think we understand the golf swing. We may feel we are swinging correctly. Trouble is, we can't *see* ourselves swing. So we need a professional observer to check us out, to note any mistakes, and put us back on track.

I cannot teach you face-to-face. But I can tell you how to get maximum benefit when you do go to someone who can. Some suggestions:

1. Realize beforehand that the teacher probably will not work a miracle with your game. You won't walk into his shop a 90 shooter and come out with a 3-handicap. You must be patient. Take delight in your good shots, but expect to hit a lot of bad ones first.

2. Explain to the instructor your golfing goals. Tell him how much time and effort you propose to spend reaching those goals. Then he'll know how to tailor his teaching to fit your aspirations and your commitment.

3. Be open-minded. Remember: *you* are the learner, not the teacher.

4. Listen carefully. Lock your attention in on the teacher's message, even when you're dying to turn away and start hitting balls. Listening is one thing; understanding is another. If your teacher is stressing proper grip, for instance, don't concern yourself with stance.

5. If you're not receiving the message, ask questions. Don't hesitate to ask what, specifically, the instructional message is supposed to accomplish. Teaching and learning is a team effort.

6. Ask your professional for a priority list of things you should work on.

7. Ask him what specific bad shots you will hit when you fail to apply his teaching. By finding out what shots result from specific

mistakes, you will be able to diagnose your failures later in practice.

8. Book a follow-up lesson to correct any misapplication of the message and to take additional instruction as the groundwork before moving on to the next stage in your advancement.

9. Practice diligently and resolutely between lessons.

To the young player: Above all else, I hope you never lose sight of the fact that golf is, indeed, a *game.* It's something to have fun doing. A good shot is something to watch and enjoy, to take a moment to savor. I sincerely hope that this little book helps to give you many such moments during your life in golf.

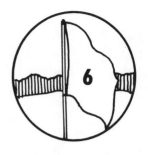

ETIQUETTE, RULES
EQUIPMENT, TERMS

Etiquette

Traditionally, golf is a gentleman's game, which means that failure to observe certain courtesies will definitely offend most of those you play with and also, at times, all others on the course. However, by observing the simple rules of etiquette that follow (excerption from The Rules of Golf, United States Golf Association, 1981), you can be assured that you will be an acceptable golfing companion, regardless of your current playing ability.

Courtesy on the Course

Consideration for Other Players

In the interest of all, players should play without delay.

No player should play until the players in front are out of range.

Players searching for a ball should signal the players behind them to pass as soon as it becomes apparent that the ball will not easily be found: they should not search for five minutes before doing so. They should not continue play until the players following them have passed and are out of range.

When the play of a hole has been completed, players should immediately leave the putting green.

Behavior During Play

No one should move, talk or stand close to or directly behind the ball or the hole when a player is addressing the ball or making a stroke.

The player who has the honor should be allowed to play before his opponent or fellow-competitor tees his ball.

Priority on the Course

In the absence of special rules, two-ball matches should have precedence of and be entitled to pass any three-or four-ball match.

A single player has no standing and should give way to a match of any kind.

Any match playing a whole round is entitled to pass a match playing a shorter round.

If a match fails to keep its place on the course and loses more than one clear hole on the players in front, it should allow the match following to pass.

Care of the Course

Holes in Bunkers

Before leaving a bunker, a player should carefully fill up and smooth over all holes and footprints made by him.

Restore Divots, Repair Ball-Marks and Damage by Spikes

Through the green, a player should ensure that any turf cut or displaced by him is replaced at once and pressed down, and that any damage to the putting green made by the ball is carefully repaired. Damage to the putting green caused by golf shoe spikes should be repaired *on completion of the hole.*

Damage to Greens — Flagsticks, Bags, etc.

Players should insure that, when putting down bags, or the flagstick, no damage is done to the putting green, and that neither they nor their caddies damage the hole by standing close to it, in handling the flagstick or in removing the ball from the hole. The flagstick should be properly replaced in the hole before the players leave the putting green. Players should not damage the putting green by leaning on their putters, particularly when removing the ball from the hole.

Golf Carts

Local Notices regulating the movement of golf carts should be strictly observed.

Damage Through Practice Swings

In taking practice swings, players should avoid causing damage to the course, particularly the tees, by removing divots.

Rules

The Rules of Golf are written and amended from time to time by the United States Golf Association and (elsewhere) by the Royal & Ancient Golf Club of St. Andrews, Scotland. These are the governing bodies of the game and set the standards, from the width of the grooves on your iron clubfaces (no wider than .035 inches) to the length of time you are permitted to look for a lost ball before continuing play at the cost of a penalty (five minutes).

The Rules are very complex. Although the Rules themselves are set forth in a small vest pocket booklet, there is a vast and continually growing volume of interpretations of these Rules. Nine out of ten golfers inadvertently break at least one Rule — and often more — in the course of a round. Nevertheless, the Rules are there to be observed and every player should become reasonably familiar with them since they will govern, beyond argument, virtually every situation you will encounter on the golf course.

I strongly recommend that you study and understand the Rules for a number of reasons. First of all, knowing the Rules will spare you the embarrassment of breaking them out of ignorance. Secondly, knowledge of the Rules can save you strokes under some circumstances by providing you with relief from perilous situations. Finally, knowing the Rules can protect you from losing an important competition since the penalties can even result in your disqualification, or at least forfeiting a hole to your opponent.

But above all, understanding and observing the Rules of Golf will earn you the respect of your fellow players and that alone makes it worth the effort of studying and digesting them. You may obtain a copy of the Rules of Golf for 50 cents from the United States Golf Association, Far Hills, N.J. 07931. It will fit nicely into the pocket of your golf bag where it should always be carried.

Ten Most Commonly Broken Rules

No. 1:
*You Don't
"Roll 'em Over"*

You play the ball as you find it, not as you'd *like* to find. There are no such things as "winter rules." Rule 16 says quite clearly, "The ball shall be played as it lies except as otherwise provided for in the Rules or Local Rules." A Local Rule may be declared when abnormal turf conditions, such as may be encountered in the winter months, may dictate the advisability of permitting "preferred lies". The purpose of that special rule is to protect the course, not to improve your golf score. Any time you move the golf ball, either with the clubhead or your hand, it costs you one penalty stroke. Okay?

95

No. 2: *The "Hand Mashie" is Illegal*

| Wrong | Right |

How many times have you found your ball tucked under a root, or peering out from among the brambles? And how many of those times have you blithely retrieved it and, with the amiable acquiescence of your playmates, tossed it back to the fairway, accepting a penalty stroke? That's naughty. You have to *play* your way back to the fairway. Rule 29 (2b-ii) sternly advises you that you may lift the unplayable ball and drop it within two club lengths, not nearer the hole — straight back as far as you like as long as you keep that point between you and the hole. The cost is only one stroke. But, if you insist on tossing the ball back into play on the fairway, you're breaking the law and it costs you *two* strokes, not *one*.

No. 3: *That Goes for One in the Water Too!*

When your shot drifts off into a watery grave it costs you the price of a golf ball and one shot to get back in the game again with a fresh ball. But what if you're one of those guys who tosses the new ball down on the fairway a good chip shot away from the boundary of the hazard? Rule 33-3b says you must measure off two club lengths from the boundary of the hazard, not nearer the hole, then drop according to the prescribed method. When you casually throw that ball back into play on the fairway you can add two more penalty strokes, making it three strokes in all.

No. 4: *Are You a Drop Flop?*

Wrong   Right

While we're on the subject, there's only one acceptable way to drop a ball back in play. You don't fling it to the ground. Rule 22-2 tells you you must stand erect, *facing the hole,* and drop the ball behind you over your shoulder. If you want to try some freestyle method of dropping the ball you can just add a penalty stroke to your score.

No. 5: *Where It Enters the Hazard, Not Where It Splashes.*

When your average, run-of-the-golf-course scofflaw sails one off into a lateral hazard (one that roughly follows the contour of the hole), he usually marks the point of splash, then proceeds to a point on land directly aligned with the splash spot — and proceeds to violate the drop rule as mentioned above. Rule 33-3b says you mark the spot where the flying ball crossed the margin on the hazard. That's where you put the new ball in play — again within two club lengths of the hazard boundary and dropped as prescribed.

No. 6: *Don't Sole Your Club in a Hazard.*

Before we leave the water hazard, let's take a look at another common No-No. If your ball lies within the staked boundaries of a hazard, your clubhead may not touch the ground or the water in the act of addressing the ball or on your backswing. In other words, you can't remove an impediment to your swing by pressing it into the ground or sweeping it out of the way with a backswing. You violate this Rule under penalty of two strokes, or thirty days in jail.

Right   Wrong

No. 7: *You Put It There; You Play It.*

All weeding should be reserved for the garden or the lawn. If you've got a lousy lie, it's just too bad. You can't uproot bushes or trample down seedlings just because they bother you. Nor can you have a confederate drag shrubbery out of your way so you can swing. Neither can you make a major haying operation out of three practice swings. That's Rule 17 and it's a two stroke rap for ignoring it.

No. 8:
The Great
O.B. Rip-Off.

Probably the most common, unwitting Rules violation occurs on the fly-away shot that leaves the course. Because of crowded course conditions and the accent on speedier play, most players prefer to toss the errant ball back into play and proceed with the game. Under the circumstances, this is understandable and tacitly condoned these days, although it is a violation of Rule 29-1. But the subsequent accounting error is unforgiveable. Saturday Morning Stanley tosses the ball back onto the course and charges himself *one stroke* penalty. Tilt! The Rule levies a stroke-and-distance penalty. That means, unless you go back and hit a second shot, the correct assessment should be *two strokes* penalty — and you lie *three* not *two*.

No. 9:
If It Moves,
You Did It.

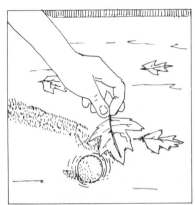

We've talked of Rules blithely fractured out of ignorance or unconcern. Now let's consider a situation where the Rules flouter may not know any better — or just may find the temptation to fudge a little too great. This is the case where a player sets up housekeeping in a rotten lie and gingerly begins removing floral debris in order to get a clean shot at the ball. And the ball moves! This is a private matter, between you and your conscience. But Rule 27-e says if the ball moves in the course of removing these "loose impediments" it's your fault and the penalty is one stroke. Just remember Bobby Jones at Worchester in the 1925 Open when his ball moved as he was addressing it. He called a penalty stroke on himself and wound up in a losing playoff with Willie MacFarlane. A bystander said he didn't see the ball move. Jones replied, "I did."

No. 10: *You Hole Out With the Ball in Play*

In baseball, football, tennis and pawnbroking you can change balls to suit your whimsy. But in golf you have to hole out with the ball you tee up — unless it is lost or becomes unfit for play. You don't pocket your scuffed ball on the green and substitute a shiny new one for putting. It just ain't cricket. And it sure ain't golf! Rule 21-1 says you must hole out with the ball driven from the teeing ground unless a Rule or Local Rule permits you to substitute another ball. It's a two-stroke penalty.

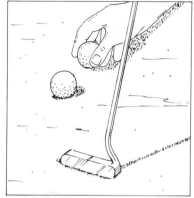

Keeping Score

The number of times you swing at the ball, plus any penalty strokes, determines your score for any given hole. The object of the game is to negotiate the 18 holes in the fewest number of strokes.

We've mentioned penalty strokes for infractions of the Rules. By far, the most common penalties occur when you lose your ball, knock it out of bounds or into a water hazard, or place it in an unplayable lie. If you understand what to do in these four situations, you may play without fear of embarrassing yourself through ignorance of the Rules.

For the lost ball and the out-of-bounds ball the Rules are identical. The penalty of each is "stroke and distance." This means you must add one penalty stroke to your score and replay the shot, thus losing the distance you had gained originally, plus the penalty stroke. To speed up play when you suspect your ball may be lost or out of bounds, you may play a "provisional" second ball. Naturally, if you find your original ball and it is not out of bounds, you will pocket the "provisional" ball and continue play with your original ball.

If your ball strays into a water hazard and you cannot or chose not to play it out, you may follow the same procedure as for the lost ball. Or, if you prefer, you may drop a fresh ball over your shoulder behind the margin of the hazard where the ball entered the water, and add a penalty stroke to your score. Usually, this is the preferred procedure. (If the ball enters a *lateral* hazard — one running the length of the fairway — you have a third option. You may drop a second ball on either side of the hazard behind the point where the original ball entered the hazard.)

In the case of an unplayable lie, you have three options. You may replay the shot. You may drop back anywhere on a line keeping the unplayable position between you and the hole. Or you may drop clear of the unplayable lie within two club lengths, not closer to the hole. In each case you must add one penalty stroke to your score.

Handicapping

Your handicap is based on the difference between your average score and the USGA course rating (not the par). As your game improves and your average score declines, your handicap also will be reduced to reflect the improvement in your game.

The handicapping system is designed to make it possible for two players of uneven ability to play on even terms by arranging for the better player to concede "handicap" strokes to the player with less ability. These strokes are allocated as indicated on the score card which ranks each hole by its degree of difficulty, ranging from 1 up to 18. In theory, the No. 1 "stroke hole" is regarded as the most difficult one on the course. The No. 18 stroke hole is the easiest.

So, if your handicap is 20 and your opponent's handicap is 12, in a handicap match he would grant you a one-stroke advantage on each of the eight low ranking stroke holes. In all probability they would be the eight longest, most treacherous holes on the golf course.

Golf Events

Whatever your reason for learning to play golf, be it merely to get outdoors and have fun or someday to win the U.S. Open, you will find your enjoyment and appreciation of the game greatly increased if you compete against others whenever possible. Even if the prize is only a small trophy or a 50-cent side bet, competition will give you added reason to meet the challenges inherent in the game and to improve your skill at it.

I've pointed out how handicaps allow even a newcomer to compete against the club champion in certain tournaments. Other events do not involve handicaps and thus do not involve the giving or taking of strokes, but are determined by gross score. However, even in these events, golfers are usually grouped with players of similar ability to ensure that everyone has a good chance to win a prize. In these events you are assigned to a group, either on the basis of your handicap or on the score you shoot in one or more qualifying rounds.

I've mentioned that stroke play tournaments are those based on total score for the round or rounds (most professional tournaments consist of four rounds at stroke play). Match play involves trying to win more holes than you lose to your opponent. If, for instance, you win four holes and your opponent wins only three, you are a "one up" winner. The match need not go the full distance. It would end, for instance, if you or your opponent were four holes "up" with only three holes left in the round.

Sometimes, in both stroke and match play, you will find yourself tied with an opponent after all holes have been completed. Generally such a tie will be broken by playing extra holes at "sudden death," until you or your opponent wins a hole. In very serious competition, however, the tournament committee will often require an 18-hole playoff. In both cases in handicap tournaments, the "stroke holes" remain the same as those originally allotted.

Not only will you find yourself playing both match play and stroke play, with or without handicaps, but also you will play in "four-ball" events (often erroneously called "foursomes" in the United States. A foursome is actually a contest between teams of two players hitting all shots alternately). Here you compete with a partner against other two-man teams, with everyone playing his own ball but only the better score of each team counting on each hole. If the competition is played with handicaps, it is the lowest "net" ball of each team that counts. The "best-ball" format is by far the most common in the United States whenever four people get together for a round of golf, and the winner is usually determined by match play — holes won and lost — rather than total strokes played for the round.

Betting

Within these basic types of competition, you will generally find yourself involved in various side games which usually involve some sort of betting. If the stakes aren't too high, these games and bets add spice and fun to the round.

Usually the amount of money involved is minimal, representing more a token of victory than a means to supplement one's income, and I strongly advise against allowing yourself to become involved in betting beyond your means, or to the point where winning or losing might create hard feelings.

The most common golf betting game is the "nassau" match. Here, individuals or teams play the first nine holes for a given prize, the second nine for a similar prize, and the overall 18 holes for the same or a slightly higher amount. The appeal of this type of bet is that it gives incentive to do well on the second nine if you may have done poorly on the first. Often, within the nassau match, you also find the element of "press" betting, whereby the player or team that is losing may "press" by asking that an additional prize — usually equal to the original amount — be awarded to the winner of the remaining holes of the nine being played.

Side betting may also involve a prize for "greenies" — for putting one's tee shot on the green and closer to the hole than that of any of the other players. "Syndicates" or "skins" or "scats" are prizes for the players whose score on a hole is lower than that of any of his fellow competitors. Frequently it will also be agreed that prizes be awarded for "birdies," a score of one under par on any hole.

Thus, within a typical group of four golfers playing together, two might be playing the other pair a nassau match, with presses allowed, plus each individual playing each of the others a nassau match, also including presses, with extra prizes awarded for any birdies and greenies. Obviously, such a battle keeps everyone interested and competitive and creates a great deal of friendly banter, both during and after the round.

There are literally dozens of other golf events and betting forms too numerous to mention here. However, if you understand these basic types you will have little or no trouble understanding the others.

Equipment

"The effectiveness of a golf club usually results much more from its influence on a player's mind than on his actual swing. For example, when I am on my game I can take clubs that are close to those I regularly use, and after a few acclimatizing shots, make them work equally well."
— *Jack Nicklaus*

Initially, you will not need a full set of clubs. A starter set which usually includes 2 woods, 4 irons and a putter should be adequate for the variety of situations you will encounter in play. The rules allow you to carry no more than 14 clubs. Most golfers today carry three or four woods and nine or ten irons, plus a putter. A popular set of woods include a No. 1 wood (known as the "driver"), a 3 wood, a 4 wood, and a 5 wood. You can include a 2 wood but, because of the 14-club limit, most people find it serves relatively little purpose. A typical set of irons will include a 2 iron, 3 iron, 4 iron, 5 iron, 6 iron, 7 iron, 8 iron, 9 iron and a fairway (pitching) wedge and a sand wedge.

In an earlier chapter I did go into detail about which clubs to use, and how to use them, for different types of shots. Now, however, the thing that I want to make very clear is that your clubs directly determine the manner in which you swing, in that, if they do not fit you properly, they will force you to a greater or lesser degree to swing incorrectly. Also, if your clubs do not match one another in certain ways, they will force you into the complicated matter of developing a slightly different swing for each differing club in the set.

For these reasons, I strongly suggest that you take some lessons from a golf pro before buying your clubs. The pro will not only improve your swing tremendously, but will thereafter fit you with clubs that match your new and improved swing pattern.

Each wood and iron club is built to hit shots of different distances and heights. The factors that produce these differences are the overall length of the club and its "loft." Loft is the degree at which the clubface slants backward when the sole of the club is set squarely on the ground.

All things being equal, the more loft you have on the face of the club, the more it will hit shots upward as opposed to forward. This is true not only because of the loft itself, but also because additional loft applies additional backspin to the ball, and additional backspin decreases distance by increasing height. Also, the greater the loft the club carries, the less forward momentum it can apply to the ball.

The distance of a shot is also affected by the overall length of the club. The longer the club, the bigger the arc on which the clubhead travels during the swing, and the bigger the arc, the greater the potential clubhead speed during impact with the ball. The greater the clubhead speed at impact, the further the ball will go if squarely struck.

Woods and irons are numbered so that you can tell at a glance which is which. The lower the number on the club, the less its loft and the greater its length. Thus, among the woods, the No. 1 wood, or "driver" is the longest-shafted and least lofted, and theoretically at least will hit shots farther than will a 3 wood, which in turn will hit longer shots than a 4 wood.

The same holds true for the irons. A 2 iron, with the lesser loft and longer shaft, will hit shots farther than will a 3 iron. Three-iron shots generally go farther than 4-iron shots, and so on, all the way up to the shortest and most-lofted club, the sand wedge, which hits shots a shorter distance in relationship to height than any other iron or wood.

The most important consideration in fitting clubs is the type of shaft selected. Shafts come in various degrees of flex, or "whippiness." Generally, the whippier the shaft, the greater your ability to "feel" the clubhead. Thus, given that you strike the ball solidly, a whippier shaft might give you slightly more distance. However, the downside to this possibility is that whippy shafts require a more precise timing of the delivery of the clubhead to the ball. This is especially true if you happen to have a relatively fast swing, in that the faster you swing, the more the whippier clubshaft will bend and twist. Therefore I generally recommend relatively stiff shafts for most men and for stronger women golfers. Weaker men and most women, I find, play better with shafts of normal flex.

Another factor is the length of the shafts. While clubs within any set vary in length to produce different types of shots, it is possible to buy full sets — or individual clubs within a set — that are longer or shorter than average. Longer clubs can produce longer shots because they allow a longer and wider swing arc, but, again, the longer the club the more difficult it is to control.

Often a golfer who is exceptionally tall or short may need clubs that are longer or shorter than average. However, factors more crucial than your height in determining club length are the length of your arms, the distance you stand from the ball, your posture at the ball, and the actual pattern of your swing. For example, it is conceivable that a 6'6" golfer with very long arms might need shorter clubs than a person of average height. If the taller person bought longer clubs, he might stand too far from the ball which, in turn, would make him swing incorrectly.

Equally important as length is the "lie" of your clubs. A club's lie is the angle formed by its head and shaft where they join. This angle is correct for you when the bottom of the club sets flat on the ground when you correctly set up to the ball in your "address position."

If you set up correctly and the outer part of the clubhead — its "toe" — doesn't rest on the ground, your club's lie is too "upright." In that case, unless you make some adjustment during your swing or stand too close to the ball, your club's "heel" will dig into the turf and cause your clubface to turn left of target during impact. The opposite clubface twisting occurs if your lie is too "flat," forcing you to either stand too far from the ball or to make some swing adjustment to avoid hitting the ball right of target by catching the turf with the club's toe.

The diameter of your grips determines how you will hold your club. Generally, grips that are too thick will make you hold the club in a way that will cause you to "slice" shots to the right if you are a righthander. Conversely, grips that are too thin may cause shots to "hook" to the left.

The weighting of your clubs is yet another factor that can influence your degree of success or failure. Clubs that are too heavy may cause you to lose clubhead speed, and thus distance, especially during the latter stages of a round when you might be tiring. Clubs that are too light for you, especially in their heads, may cause a loss of "feel," and thereby a reduced sense of "rhythm" and "timing." The trend today is toward lighter clubshafts and, thus, to lighter overall club weight. But clubs that are *too* light can cause you to swing too fast at the wrong part of your swing.

Most manufacturers make various types of balls, even though they may all look alike, and the type you use is largely a matter of personal taste. There are golf balls made entirely of solid materials that do not cut; balls made of tightly wound rubber and covered with cut-resistant material; tightly wound balls with thin covers that do cut easily, and so on. Inexperienced players who mishit many shots generally prefer the non-cuttable or cut-resistant balls, while most better players prefer the "feel" and flight characteristics of thin-covered, wound-rubber balls.

Balls are graded by their "compression." A 70 compression ball will "flatten" to a greater extent on the clubface during impact than will an 80 compression ball, which will, in turn, be softer than a 90 or 100 compression ball.

Many golfers prefer a lower compression ball because it feels "softer" when struck. As a rule, however, the higher the ball's compression, the farther it will go, even though it will not compress so readily. I suggest that you use a high-compression ball for maximum distance, but not so high that it feels rock hard when struck. Even many touring professionals prefer balls of slightly less than top compression, either because their extra flattening allows the application of more backspin or sidespin, or simply because they "feel" better at impact.

Any golf professional will advise you about which brands of balls are high or low compression. Whichever you select, however, I suggest that you always buy top quality, because the difference in price between the best and the cheapy is minimal when compared to your overall golfing expenses, but the difference in terms of distance and general playability is considerable.

Golf shoes and gloves are vital if you are to play up to your full potential. You need the spikes for footwork and balance as you swing, and the glove for maximum control over the club. Without both you cannot swing as freely and fully as you might.

Gloves are generally worn only on the righthander's left hand and the lefthander's right hand. Buy the most expensive glove you can find in your pro shop. It will cost you two or three dollars more than the cheapest, and it will be thinner, more durable and less susceptible to stretching. Ask the golf shop attendant to help you find one that fits properly — which means very snugly.

Golf bags come in myriad types, sizes, colors, and qualities. I suggest you consider these points before buying:

• A big, durable bag lasts longer, protects clubs better, and holds more miscellaneous equipment — even shoes and laundry — when you travel to play golf.

• A smaller, lighter bag costs less and saves you or your caddie wear and tear.

Many avid golfers buy both the first type — as a long-term investment, and for travel, tournament play and storing extra clothing when wet or cold weather threatens — and the second, lighter bag for everyday play in nice weather. I suggest, however, that you avoid bags that are so cheaply made that they jam your clubs together, allow rain or dew to soak through, or lack sufficient support and balance for easy carrying.

In addition to the above, you will need tees, a golf umbrella, a windbreaker jacket, a box of stretchable band-aids for sore hands and fingers, and possibly suntan lotion and a golf hat. Personally, I feel a hat is a must to protect you from sunstroke on hot days and to ease the sun's glare, which can make judging distance extremely difficult. If you plan to play a lot of golf and to enter tournaments, you will find a rain suit invaluable for those wet and cold days when you must forge ahead.

Advice For Juniors

If you are under 5'4'' tall, or if you are not as strong as a normal 15-year-old, standard adult clubs will probably be too long or too heavy for you to swing easily, leading to bad playing habits. Instead, go for a full set of junior-sized clubs.

If you are just starting golf, you might ask your father or your club professional to cut down a secondhand set of clubs to fit your size. If you find that you like golf, and if you can afford new junior clubs, you should buy a set of these when you get to be 11 or 12 years old. If you cannot afford a full set of 14 clubs, get one that includes one or two woods, about four irons, and a putter. That set may last you until you are big and strong — and wealthy — enough to buy a full set of adult clubs.

Since you will probably be carrying your own bag, don't get one that is too heavy. I do suggest that you use golf shoes and a golf glove, but if your feet are growing rapidly you probably should not buy expensive shoes.

Finally, be sure you understand all the rules of etiquette in this chapter. On a golf course you should always act like an adult — just as if you were Jack Nicklaus.

A COLLECTION OF GOLFING TERMS

The following is a collection of golfing terms. As in other chapters of this book, any definitions involving the words "clockwise" or "counterclockwise," and "right" and "left" in the directional or anatomical sense, are presented as they would apply to righthanded golfers.

1. Ace

Playing a hole in one stroke. Also a "hole-in-one."

2. Address

The position of the player at the ball before swinging.

3. Addressing the Ball *

A player has "addressed the ball" when he has taken his stance (Definition 199) and has also grounded his club, except that in a hazard a player has addressed the ball when he has taken his stance.

4. Advice *

"Advice" is any counsel or suggestion which could influence a player in determining his play, the choice of a club, or the method of making a stroke.

5. Air Shot

See "whiff."

6. Angle of Attack

Steepness of clubhead's path of approach to the ball on the forward swing.

7. Approach

A shot to a green not made from the teeing area. Also, the area in front of the green.

8. Apron

Grassy area immediately adjacent to a green, usually cut shorter than fairway grass but longer than the grass on the green itself.

9. Away

Designation for ball or its owner farthest from flagstick and thus next in turn to play.

10. Back Door

Side of cup farthest from player.

11. Back Nine

Second nine holes of an 18-hole course.

12. Backspin

Reverse spin imparted to ball when struck.

13. Ball Deemed to Move *

A ball is deemed to have "moved" if it leaves its position and comes to rest in any other place.

14. Ball Holed *

A ball is "holed" when it lies within the circumference of the hole and all of it is below the level of the lip of the hole.

15. Ball in Play, Provisional Ball, Wrong Ball *

a. A ball is "in play" as soon as the player has made a stroke on the teeing ground. It remains as his ball in play until holed out, except when it is out of bounds, lost or lifted, or another ball has been substituted under an applicable Rule or Local Rule: a ball so substituted becomes the ball in play.

b. A "provisional ball" is a ball played under Rule 30 for a ball which may be lost outside a water hazard or may be out of bounds. It ceases to be a provisional ball when the Rule provides *either* that the player continue play with it as the ball in play *or* that it be abandoned.

c. A "wrong ball" is any ball other than the ball in play or a provisional ball or, in stroke play, a second ball played under Rule 11-5 or under Rule 21-3d.

16. Ball Lost *

A ball is "lost" if:

a. It be not found, or be not identified as his by the player, within five minutes after the player's side or his or their caddies have begun to search for it; *or*

b. The player has put another ball into play under the Rules, even though he may not have searched for the original ball; *or*

c. The player has played any stroke with a provisional ball from a point nearer the hole than the place where the original ball is likely to be, whereupon the provisional ball becomes the ball in play.

Time spent in playing a wrong ball is not counted in the five minute period allowed for search.

17. Banana Ball

Slang for a shot that curves from left to right.

18. Bent

A finely-textured species of grass.

19. Bermuda

A coarsely-textured species of grass.

20. Best-Ball

A match in which one golfer plays against the better ball of two players or the best ball of three players. (Term is commonly misapplied to ''four-ball'' matches).

21. Birdie

A score of one stroke under par on a hole.

22. Bite

Backspin sufficient to make ball stop quickly, or actually bounce and roll backwards, upon landing.

23. Blade

To catch back side of ball with leading edge of iron club and cause a low, driving shot. Also describes a thin, metal-headed putter.

24. Blast

Type of bunker shot in which clubhead displaces a relatively large amount of sand.

25. Blind Bogey

Competition in which player estimates before starting what handicap will be needed to put his net score between 70 and 80, and thus qualify him for a blind drawing of a winning number in that range.

26. Blind Hole

One on which green cannot be seen by player making a normal approach shot.

27. Blind Shot

Approach shot on which golfer cannot see the flagstick.

28. Bogey

One stroke over par on a given hole. In Great Britain, sometimes used as the number of strokes a better-than-average golfer is expected to take on a hole.

29. Borrow

The amount a player allows for a putt to curve sideways on a slanted green.

30. Bounce

The extension below horizontal of a portion of a club's sole; usually in the case of the sand wedge.

31. Brassie

The No. 2 wood.

32. Break

The sideways curving of a shot as it rolls on the green.

33. Bunker
A sand hazard, commonly called a "trap."

34. Bye
Situation in match play where a competitor has no opponent, because of insufficient number of qualifiers, and thus advances automatically to next round of play.

35. Caddie
Someone who carries a player's clubs, who may perform various other services, and who has the right to give advice to the player and his side.

36. Caddie, Forecaddie and Equipment *
a. A "caddie" is one who carries or handles a players' clubs during play and otherwise assists him in accordance with the Rules.

When one caddie is employed by more than one player, he is always deemed to be the caddie of the player whose ball is involved, and equipment carried by him is deemed to be that player's equipment, except when the caddie acts upon specific directions of another player, in which case he is considered to be that other player's caddie.

Note: In threesome, foursome, best-ball and four-ball play, a caddie carrying for more than one player should be assigned to the members of one side.

b. A "forecaddie" is one employed by the Committee to indicate to players the position of balls on the course, and is an outside agency (Definition 146).

c. "Equipment" is anything used, worn or carried by or for the player except his ball in play. Equipment includes a golf cart. If such a cart is shared by more than one player, its status under the Rules is the same as that of a caddie employed by more than one player.

37. Carry
The distance between ball's original position and where it lands.

38. Cast
To uncock or straighten the wrists prematurely in the downswing.

39. Casual Water
"Casual water" is any temporary accumulation of water which is visible before or after the player takes his stance and is not in a water hazard. Snow and ice are either casual water or loose impediments, at the option of the player.

40. Chip Shot
Short approach shot of low trajectory, usually involving minimal

carry and maximum bounce and roll.

41. Close Lie

Ball setting down in grass or otherwise close to ground's surface. Also called a "tight lie."

42. Closed Face

Clubface aimed left of intended line at address or on impact. Also, a position during the swing that is likely to produce a closed face at impact.

43. Closed Stance

Left foot closer than right foot to intended line of flight.

44. Closed Alignment

Positioning of left side closer than right side to intended line of flight.

45. Clubface

Normal striking surface of the clubhead.

46. Collar

Grass around the edges of a green or hazard.

47. Committee *

The "Committee" is the committee in charge of the competition or, if the matter does not arise in a competition, the committee in charge of the course.

48. Competitor *

A "competitor" is a player in a stroke competition. A "fellow-competitor" is any person with whom the competitor plays. Neither is partner of the other.

In stroke play foursome and four-ball competitions, where the context so admits, the word "competitor" or "fellow-competitor" shall be held to include his partner.

49. Course *

The "course" is the whole area within which play is permitted. It is the duty of the Committee to define its boundaries accurately.

50. Course Rating

The score a zero handicap ("scratch") golfer should make when playing well under normal conditions, as determined by a golf association for figuring handicaps of those who play the course in question.

51. Cup

Metal or plastic lining fitted into the hole.

52. Cuppy

Lie in which the ball sets in a depression.

53. Cut Shot
Stroke applying a clockwise spin to the ball that causes it to curve from left to right.

54. Divot
Turf uprooted by clubhead during the swing.

55. Dogleg
A hole with a fairway that bends to the left or right.

56. Dormie
Situation in match play wherein a player or a side is ahead by as many holes as remain to be played.

57. Double Bogey
Two strokes over par on a hole.

58. Double Eagle
Three strokes under par on a hole.

59. Down
The number of holes a player or a side is behind in a match.

60. Draw
A shot that starts on the intended line and then curves slightly to the left.

61. Drive
Shot made with a driver from the teeing ground.

62. Driving Iron
Club with the approximate loft of a No. 1 iron.

63. Drop
The act of a player facing a hole being played, standing upright, and dropping his ball over his shoulder on occasions when allowed or required to do so by the Rules of Golf.

64. Dub
A bad shot. Also, a poor golfer.

65. Duck Hook
A shot that nosedives and curves abruptly to the left.

66. Duffer
A poor player. Also called a "hacker" or a "dub."

67. Eagle
Two strokes under par on a hole.

68. Explosion
See "blast."

69. Face
See "clubface."

70. Fade

A shot that starts on the intended line and then curves slightly to the right.

71. Fairway

Area between teeing ground and green that is regularly mowed and otherwise prepared with special care.

72. Feather

To hit an intentionally high shot that curves gently from left to right, and that stops quickly upon landing.

73. Finesse

To deliberately play other than a standard shot, in overcoming obstacles, weather, ground conditions, and the like. Also called "type" shots.

74. Flagstick *

The "flagstick" is a movable straight indicator provided by the Committee, with or without bunting or other material attached, centered in the hole to show its position. It shall be circular in cross-section.

75. Flashing

Uncocking the wrists and flipping the clubhead with the hands early in the downswing.

76. Flat Lie

A more obtuse angle than normal between the sole and the shaft of a club.

77. Flat Plane

A characteristic of a swing that is less upright, or shallower, than normal.

78. Flight Path

See "intended line."

79. Follow-Through

The portion of the swing occurring after ball has left clubface.

80. Fore

Warning cry shouted to player(s) in danger of being struck by a shot.

81. Forecaddie

Person positioned down the fairway to spot and mark position of players' shots.

82. Forward Press

Slight movement of some part of the anatomy, usually the hands, more or less toward the target immediately prior to starting the backswing.

83. Four-Ball

Match in which two people play their better ball against the better ball of two others. (Frequently mislabeled "best-ball.")

84. Foursome

A match in which two golfers play against two others and each side plays one ball, stroking alternately. Also, in North America, the common term for a group of four players.

85. Free Drop

A "drop" in which no penalty is incurred.

86. Fringe

See "apron."

87. Frog Hair

See "apron."

88. Front Nine

First nine holes of an 18-hole course.

89. Gimme

Slang term for a putt conceded to an opponent in match play.

90. Grain

Flat-lying grass, usually on a green, that tends to pull shots in the direction it lies.

91. Green

Closely-cut area of the course that contains the hole, cup, and flagstick.

92. Greenies

A form of gambling in which all players pay a set amount to the one whose tee shot finishes on the green and closest to the hole.

93. Grip

The covered portion of the clubshaft that is held in the hands. Also, the player's grasp of the club.

94. Gross Score

Actual score shot on a hole, or for a round, with no handicap strokes deducted.

95. Ground Under Repair

"Ground under repair" is any portion of the course so marked by order of the Committee or so declared by its authorized representative. It includes material piled for removal and a hole made by a greenkeeper, even if not so marked. Stakes and lines defining ground under repair are in such ground.

Note: *Grass cuttings and other material left on the course which have been abandoned and are not intended to be removed are not ground under repair unless so marked.*

96. Half or Halve

A tied hole in match play.

97. Handicap

A number indicating a golfer's skill. Based on 85 percent (96 percent after December 31, 1975) of the average of the ten lowest differences, from his last 20 rounds, between his gross score and the rating of the course where it was shot.

98. Handicap Strokes

Shots deducted from a player's score to determine his or her standing in a stroke play competition. Or, shots deducted from the score of the higher handicap player on designated holes (see "stroke holes") in match play competition.

99. Hanging Lie

A ball at rest on a severe downslope.

100. Hazards *

A "hazard" is any bunker, water hazard or lateral water hazard. Bare patches, scrapes, roads, tracks and paths are not hazards.

It is the duty of the Committee to define accurately the extent of the water hazards. That part of a water hazard to be played as a lateral water hazard should be distinctively marked. Stakes and lines defining the margins of hazards are in the hazards.

a. A "bunker" is an area of bare ground, often a depression, which is usually covered with sand. Grass-covered ground bordering or within a bunker is *not* part of the hazard.

b. A "water hazard" is any sea, lake, pond, river, ditch, surface drainage ditch or other open water course (regardless of whether or not it contains water), and anything of a similar nature. All ground or water within the margin of a water hazard, whether or not it be covered with any growing substance, is part of the water hazard. The margin of a water hazard is deemed to extend vertically upwards.

c. A "lateral water hazard" is a water hazard or that part of a water hazard so situated that it is not possible or is deemed by the Committee to be impracticable to drop a ball behind the water hazard and keep the spot at which the ball last crossed the margin of the hazard between the player and the hole.

117

Note: *Water hazards should be defined by yellow stakes or lines and lateral water hazards by red stakes or lines.*

101. Head

The striking portion at the end of the club.

102. Heel

The part of the clubface nearest that shaft. Also, a shot struck on this portion of the face.

103. High Side

Area above the hole on a sloping green.

104. Hole *

The "hole" shall be 4¼ inches in diameter and at least 4 inches deep. If a lining be used, it shall be sunk at least 1 inch below the putting green surface unless the nature of the soil makes it impractical to do so; its outer diameter shall not exceed 4¼ inches.

105. Hole-High

A shot to a green that finishes even with the hole but off to one side.

106. Hole-in-One

First shot of a hole when it finishes in the cup. Also called an "ace."

107. Hole Out

To make a stroke that puts the ball into the cup.

108. Honor *

The side which is entitled to play first from the teeing ground is said to have the "honor."

109. Hood

To decrease the effective loft of the clubface at address by tilting its top edge forward. Also sometimes used in referring to a closed clubface.

110. Hook

A shot that curves from right to left as a result of the clubface looking to the left of its path of movement on impact, and thus imparting counterclockwise sidespin.

111. Hosel

The part of an iron clubhead into which the shaft fits.

112. Inside-Out

Clubhead movement across the intended line from left to right during impact.

113. Inside the Line

The area on player's side of the intended line as he or she addresses the ball and swings.

114. Intended Line

The path along which a player plans for a shot to travel. Also called "target line."

115. Interlock

Type of grip in which the left forefinger and right little finger intertwine.

116. Irons

Clubs with heads made primarily of metal, but not including putters.

117. Lag

Putt played primarily to finish near hole rather than actually in it.

118. Lay Back

The act of increasing the effective loft of the clubface by tilting its top edge backward.

119. Lie

The position of the ball in relation to its immediate surroundings. Also, the angle formed by the club's sole and shaft.

120. Links

Grounds laid out for playing golf; a golf course.

121. Lip

The edge of the hole. Also, a putt that rims the hole but stays out.

122. Loft

The degrees at which a clubface lies back from vertical.

123. Loose Impediments *

The term "loose impediments" denotes natural objects not fixed or growing and not adhering to the ball, and includes stones not solidly embedded, leaves, twigs, branches and the like, dung, worms and insects and casts or heaps made by them.

Snow and ice are either casual water or loose impediments, at the option of the player.

Sand and loose soil are loose impediments on the putting green, but not elsewhere on the course.

124. Low Side

Area below the hole on a slanted area of green.

125. Loop

Shifting the hands outward or inward near the top of the back swing so that the plane of the downswing becomes steeper or shallower than that of the backswing.

126. Marker

A "marker" is a scorer in stroke play who is appointed by the Committee to record a competitor's score. He may be a fellow-competitor. He is not a referee.

A marker should not lift a ball or mark its position unless authorized to do so by the competitor and, unless he is a fellow-competitor, should not attend the flagstick or stand at the hole or mark its position.

127. Mashie

Iron club with the approximate loft of a No. 5 iron.

128. Match

A contest between two players, or a player and a side, or two sides, which is determined by the number of holes won or lost.

129. Match Play

Competition conducted under rules governing matches.

130. Medal

The lowest of all qualifying scores (derives from traditional prizes of medals awarded in amateur golf).

131. Medalist

The person with the lowest qualifying score.

132. Medal Play

Colloquialism for competition based on the total number of strokes taken. Correct usage is "stroke play."

133. Mid-Iron

Iron club with the approximate loft of a No. 2 iron.

134. Mulligan

A second attempt at a shot, sometimes allowed in friendly games. Usually taken on the first tee. Not recognized by Rules of Golf.

135. Nassau

Betting competition in which stakes are wagered on the outcome of the first nine holes, second nine holes, and the entire 18.

136. Neck

That part of any club where the shaft joins the head.

137. Net

Score for a hole or a round after handicap strokes are deducted.

138. Niblick

Club with the approximate loft of a No. 8 iron.

139. Observer *

An "observer" is appointed by the Committee to assist a referee to decide questions of fact and to report to him any breach of a Rule or Local Rule. An observer should not attend the flagstick, stand at or mark the position of the hole, or lift the ball or mark its position.

140. Obstructions *

An "obstruction" is anything artificial, whether erected, placed or left on the course, including the artificial surfaces and sides of roads and paths but excepting: —

a. Objects defining out of bounds, such as walls, fences, stakes and railings;

b. In water hazards, artificially surfaced banks or beds, including bridge supports when part of such a bank. Bridges and bridge supports which are not part of such a bank are obstructions;

c. Any obstruction declared by the Committee to be an integral part of the course.

141. Open Face

Clubface aimed right of intended line at address or on impact. Also refers to a clubface position during the swing that is likely to produce an open face at impact.

142. Open Stance

Right foot closer than left to intended line of flight. Same applies to "open shoulders," "open hips," and the like.

143. Open Tournament

Competition in which both amateurs and professionals are eligible. Or any tournament conducted on an open entry rather than an invitational basis.

144. Out of Bounds

"Out of bounds" is ground on which play is prohibited.

When out of bounds is fixed by stakes or a fence, the out of bounds line is determined by the nearest inside points of the stakes or fence posts at ground level; the line is deemed to extend vertically upwards. When out of bounds is fixed by a line on the ground, the line itself is out of bounds.

A ball is out of bounds when all of it lies out of bounds.

145. Out-of-Bounds Shot

Stroke that finishes in an out-of-bounds area. Shot must be replayed from original position, thus sacrificing distance gained, with one penalty stroke added.

146. Outside Agency *

An "outside agency" is any agency not part of the match or, in stroke play, not part of a competitor's side, and includes a referee, a marker, an observer, or a forecaddie employed by the Committee. Neither wind nor water is an outside agency.

147. Outside-In

Clubhead movement across intended line from right to left during impact.

148. Outside the Line

The area on the opposite side of the intended target line as a player addresses the ball and swings.

149. Over the Top

Incorrectly starting the downswing by turning the right shoulder around, as if throwing sidearm, instead of swinging it under. Generally causes outside-in clubhead path and ultra-steep angle of attack.

150. Overlap

Grip type in which right little finger laps over left forefinger. Popularized by the late Harry Vardon, thus also called "Vardon" grip.

151. Par

Score an expert would be expected to make on a hole, including the allowance of two putts on the green.

U.S.G.A. YARDAGE FOR GUIDANCE

Par	Men	Par	Women
3	Up to 250 Yds.	3	Up to 210 Yds.
4	251-470 Yds.	4	211-400 Yds.
5	471 and over	5	401-575 Yds.
		6	576 and over

152. Partner *

A "partner" is a player associated with another player on the same side.

In a threesome, foursome or a four-ball where the context so admits, the word "player" shall be held to include his partner.

153. Penalty Stroke *

A "penalty stroke" is one added to the score of a side under certain Rules. It does not affect the order of play.

154. Pin-High

See "hole-high."

155. Pitch

Approach shot of high trajectory made with a highly-lofted club that settles relatively quickly upon landing.

156. Pitch-and-Run

Shot played with an iron so that it flies lower than normal and runs readily forward upon landing.

157. Pitching Wedge

Short-shafted iron club that is second only to sand wedge in its degree of loft.

158. Pivot

The turning of the body during the swing.

159. Play Through

An invitation given by a slower-playing group to let the following group go ahead by "playing through" as the slow group stands aside.

160. Plugged Lie

Ball at rest in the indentation it made upon landing.

161. Preferred Lies

Easing of the rules that allows player to move ball to a better position in the fairway when course conditions are substandard. Not recognized in Rules of Golf. Also called "winter rules."

162. Press

An extra bet, usually equal to the original amount, requested by a losing player. Also refers to an effort to gain extra distance by applying more force than necessary in swinging. (See also "forward press.")

163. Provisional Ball

A second ball played from the same spot as the original when the first ball is suspected of being lost or out of bounds.

164. Pull

A shot that travels more or less on a straight line but to the left of the player's intended line.

165. Punch Shot

An intentionally low shot resulting from the hands' leading the clubhead through impact and thus decreasing the club's effective loft.

166. Push

A shot that flies more or less straight but to the right of the player's intended line.

167. Putt

Stroke made on the green with a putter.

168. Putter

Least-lofted club in the bag; usually used for rolling ball on the green.

169. Putting Green *

The "putting green" is all ground of the hole being played which is specially prepared for putting or otherwise defined as such by the Committee.

A ball is deemed to be on the putting green when any part of it touches the putting green.

170. Reading the Green

Determining the line a shot — usually a putt — will seemingly take on the putting surface.

171. Reading the Putt

See "reading the green."

172. Referee *

A "referee" is a person who has been appointed by the Committee to accompany players to decide questions of fact and of golf law. He shall act on any breach of Rule or Local Rule which he may observe or which may be reported to him by an observer (Definition 139).

In stroke play the Committee may limit a referee's duties.

A referee should not attend the flagstick, stand at or mark the position of the hole, or lift the ball or mark its position.

173. Release

The act of freely swinging the arms down and forward and uncocking the wrists without inhibition as the body unwinds.

174. Rim

The edge of the hole. Also, causing a ball to roll around the edge of the hole without falling in.

175. Rhythm

The variation in speed of movement within one's swing. The "beat" of the swing within its overall pace or tempo.

176. Rough

Area of the course that is not considered fairway, green, or hazard; usually unmowed and relatively unkempt.

177. Round

The playing of the holes of a course in proper sequence. A "stipulated round" is 18 holes unless otherwise authorized by the local committee.

178. Round Robin
Competition in which every player or side competes against every other player or side once.

179. Rub of the Green *
A "rub of the green" occurs when a ball in motion is accidentally stopped or deflected by any outside agency.

180. Sand Trap
Common term for "bunker." A hazard filled with sand.

181. Scratch Play
Competition in which no handicap strokes are awarded.

182. Scratch Player
Golfer with a handicap of zero.

183. Scuff
To contact ground before the ball on one's forward stroke.

184. Setup
See "address."

185. Shaft
The elongated portion of the club to which the grip and clubhead are attached.

186. Shaft Flex
The built-in degree to which a shaft will bend under a given amount of pressure.

187. Shank
A shot that flies to the right of the intended line, due to being contacted on the neck or hosel of the club rather than on the clubface.

188. Short Game
Pitching, chipping, and putting.

189. Sides and Matches *
SIDE: A player, or two or more players who are partners.

SINGLE: A match in which one plays against another.

THREESOME: A match in which one plays against two, and each side plays one ball.

FOURSOME: A match in which two play against two, and each side plays one ball.

THREE-BALL: A match in which three play against one another, each playing his own ball.

BEST-BALL: A match in which one plays against the better ball of two or the best ball of three players.

FOUR-BALL: A match in which two play their better ball against the better ball of two other players.

Note: *In a best-ball or four-ball match, if a partner be absent for reasons satisfactory to the Committee, the remaining member(s) of his side may represent the side.*

190. Skin

See "syndicates."

191. Skull

See "blade."

192. Sky

To mishit a shot so that the ball flies higher and shorter than expected.

193. Slice

A shot that curves sharply from left to right of the intended line because of clockwise sidespin resulting from the clubface being open to the clubhead path during impact.

194. Sole

The bottom of the clubhead. Also, the act of placing the club on the ground at address.

195. Spoon

The No. 3 wood.

196. Square Face

Clubface aimed down intended line at address or on impact. Also refers to a clubface position during the swing that is likely to produce a square face during impact.

197. Square Position

A straightline relationship formed by the back of the left hand, wrist, and forearm.

198. Square Stance

Both feet equidistant from intended target line. Same applies to "square shoulders," and "square hips" — each equidistant from, or aligned parallel to, the intended target.

199. Stance *

Taking the "stance" consists in a player placing his feet in position for and preparatory to making a stroke.

200. Stiff

Shot finishing very close to flagstick.

201. Stipulated Round *

The "stipulated round" consists of playing the holes of the course in their correct sequence unless otherwise authorized by the Committee. The number of holes in a stipulated round is 18 unless a smaller number is authorized by the Committee.

In match play only, the Committee may, for the purpose of settling a tie, extend the stipulated round to as many holes as are required for a match to be won.

202. Stony

See "stiff."

203. Stroke *

A "stroke" is the forward movement of the club made with the intention of fairly striking at and moving the ball.

204. Stroke Holes

Holes on which, in match play, the higher handicap player or side receives a net score.

205. Stroke Play

Competition decided by the sum of the strokes taken by a player or his side.

206. Sudden Death

Additional competition played over extra holes until a winner is determined from among those tied at the end of regulation play.

207. Swingweight

A measurement reflecting the weight distribution of a club's various components as determined on a swingweight scale. Used primarily for matching clubs within a set so that they feel the same when swung.

208. Syndicates

A form of gambling in which a set amount is paid by all players to the player who scores the lowest score on a hole.

209. Takeaway

Initial part of the backswing.

210. Target Line

An imaginary line extending from the golfer's target back to and through and beyond his ball.

211. Tee

The small peg on which the ball is usually set and from which it is played on the opening shot of the hole. (See also, "teeing ground.")

212. Teeing *

In "teeing," the ball may be placed on the ground, on an irregularity of surface created by the player on the ground or on sand or other substance in order to raise it off the ground.

213. Tee Shot
The first shot played on a hole.

214. Teeing Ground *
The "teeing ground" is the starting place for the hole to be played. It is a rectangular area two club-lengths in depth, the front and the sides of which are defined by the outside limits of two tee-markers. A ball is outside the teeing ground when all of it lies outside the stipulated area.

When playing the first stroke with any ball (including a provisional ball) from the teeing ground, the tee-markers are immovable obstructions (Definition 140).

215. Teeing Up
The act of placing the ball on a tee. Sometimes used colloquially for the act of playing golf, as in "Let's tee it up."

216. Tempo
The overall pace of a player's golf swing.

217. Terms Used in Reckoning in Match Play *
In match play, the reckoning of holes is kept by the terms: — so many "holes up" or "all square," and so many "to play."

A side is "dormie" when it is as many holes up as there are holes remaining to be played.

218. Texas Wedge
Slang expression referring to the putter when used for shots from off the green.

219. Three-Ball
A match in which three play against one another, each playing his own ball.

220. Threesome
A match in which one plays against two, and each side plays one ball. Generally used in North America to designate a three-ball.

221. Through the Green *
"Through the green" is the whole area of the course except: —
a. Teeing ground and putting green of the hole being played;
b. All hazards on the course.

222. Timing
The sequence of movement of various parts of the body during the swing.

223. Toe
Part of the clubhead farthest from the shaft. Also, the act of con-

tacting the ball with that portion of the clubhead.

224. Top

Shot in which the leading edge or bottom of the club's sole contacts the ball above its center.

225. Trap

See "sand trap." Also, the act of contacting the ball when the clubhead is still moving downward.

226. Types of Club ˙

There are three recognized types of golf club: —

An "iron" club is one with a head which usually is relatively narrow from face to back, and usually is made of steel.

A "wood" club is one with a head relatively broad from face to back, and usually is made of wood, plastic or a light metal.

A "putter" is a club designed primarily for use on the putting green — seen Definition 169.

227. Upright Lie

A more acute angle than normal between the sole and the shaft of a club.

228. Upright Plane

A characteristic of a swing that is steeper than normal.

229. Unplayable Lie

A ball not in a water hazard that is deemed unplayable by its owner because of its positioning.

230. Vardon Grip

See "overlap."

231. Waggle

Clubhead movement at address prior to swinging.

232. Whiff

A stroke in which the clubhead fails to make any contact with the ball.

233. Whipping

Thread or twine used to wrap the area where the head and shaft of the club join.

234. Winter Rules

See "preferred lies."

235. Woods

Clubs with heads made primarily of wood, excepting putters.

SELECTED PERIODICALS

Golf
> 380 Madison Avenue
> New York, New York 10017

Golf Digest
> 495 Westport Avenue
> Norwalk, Connecticut 06856

The Golf Journal
> United States Golf Association
> Far Hills, New Jersey 07931

Golf World
> Box 2000
> Southern Pines, North Carolina 28387

Journal of Health, Physical Education and Recreation
> American Association for Health, Physical Education
> and Recreation
> 1201 Sixteenth Street
> Washington, D.C. 20036

Professional Golfer
> Professional Golfers' Association of America
> Box 12458
> Lake Park, Florida 33403

USGA Journal and Turf Management
> United States Golf Association
> Far Hills, New Jersey 07931

RULES, HANDICAPPING AND COMPETITION

Easy Way to Learn Golf Rules (current year)
National Golf Foundation
200 Castlewood Drive
North Palm Beach, Florida 33408

The Rules of Golf (current year)
U.S.G.A. Golf Handbook (current year)
Golf Rules in Pictures (current year)
United States Golf Association
Golf House
Far Hills, N.J. 07931

The New Golf Mind, Wiren, Coop, with Sheehan
Golf Digest Book Service
495 Westport Ave.
Westport, CT. 16856